The Gift of Leadership:

How to Relight the Volunteer Spirit in the 21st Century

by Mark Levin, CAE

ISBN 0-9660080-1-4

Third printing, February, 1999
Fourth Printing, December, 1999
Fifth Printing, July, 2000
Sixth Printing, July, 2001
Seventh Printing, June, 2002

B.A.I., Inc.
10015 Old Columbia Road
Suite B-215
Columbia, MD 21046
Ph: 301-596-2584
Fax: 301-596-2594
www.baileadership.com

For Jennie and Brian,

and

winktas and gigis,

and

all the love there is

Spreading the Wealth

Doug MacDonald dedicated his adult life to helping those who were in need of assistance to continue their educational experiences. Doug was a graduate of Toledo University, and received a Doctorate in Higher Education Administration from George Washington University. He served as Director of Financial Aid at the University of Delaware and as head the Maryland State Scholarship Board.

Throughout his career, Doug was active in many volunteer organizations, often as President or in another leadership role. Doug knew and understood the Gift of Leadership, and he not only received it but gave it many, many times.

Doug MacDonald died of cancer just before his 48th birthday. In 1995, the Douglas S. MacDonald Memorial Fund was established to provide scholarships to disadvantaged students. A portion of the purchase price of each copy of *"The Gift of Leadership"* will be donated to this fund.

Table of Contents

FORWARD

Volunteer?

Leader?

Are they the same?

Not really. That's not what this book is all about. It's not about definitions or stereotypes. It's about *using* the leadership experience to help volunteers - and volunteer organizations - be more effective.

There will always be a group of people who are willing to volunteer to help an organization but have no desire to attain any of the traditional "leadership" positions. That doesn't mean that they can't benefit from their volunteer experience. In fact, that's the best way to attract and keep a growing number of volunteers. Give them an experience where they feel they take as much away from their volunteer role as they put into it, and they will not only come back to serve again they will bring others with them!

We hope that this book will do two things: encourage people to volunteer by showing them how important the work of volunteers and volunteer organizations is and give them the confidence that they can carry out their volunteer and leadership responsibilities at the highest possible level. If you want to simplify that to say "motivate" volunteers and "train" them to be successful leaders, that's fine.

The intent is to share the experiences of volunteer leaders in thousands of organizations around the world. Their ability to lead their organizations to greater accomplishments is due in large part to their understanding of the Gift of Leadership.

They know what the Gift has meant to them, and they know how the Gift can help others.

In Russia, there is an organization that is dedicated to helping women who worked for the government under the previous Communist regime to better market themselves in the struggling democracy. These women, many of whom are professionals with advanced degrees in engineering and medicine, have never had to look for jobs before. They had their entire educations paid for by their government and had always been assured of lifetime employment in one of the many layers of the old Soviet system. Through this volunteer organization, they are being trained not only to find jobs but also how to develop skills they will need for whatever jobs they find. The organization is also representing these women to various governmental agencies who may have funds available to assist in the retraining of this valuable work force. In many ways, this organization is the personification of many of the ways that volunteer groups meet a need in society. It also shows the importance of the Gift of Leadership.

In South Africa a similar organization exists. In this organization a group of volunteers is teaching young women how to sew dresses and other fashion items, as well as how to set up small businesses to sell their creations. By doing so, the organization not only empowers the women it is helping, it also provides a valuable experience for the volunteer leaders who do the work of the organization. Everyone benefits from an organization like this one - the women, the organization, and the South African economy and society.

In the United States, there is camp for children suffering from cancer. The camp is free to these children and their parents, and thousands of children have lived a better life because of their involvement with the camp. Much of the work to build the camp was done by volunteers, and the governing Board of the foundation that started the camp is made up entirely of volunteers. During the camp season hundreds of young people volunteer to work at the camp. They are all volunteers, but they are not all leaders - yet. Even those who don't seek leadership are exposed to it and that, in itself, becomes a part of their volunteer experience.

All of these examples of volunteer organizations doing important work reinforces how critical it is to keep the volunteer spirit alive and growing in the next century. It would be easy to fall into the trap of letting the pressure of time and the convenience of technology convince us that volunteer activities are no longer necessary or practical. That would also be the biggest mistake that could be made. Volunteers, and volunteer organizations, are still among the best resources available to make this a better world.

These individuals and organizations give us a vehicle for moving ahead. We owe it to the volunteers to give them the Gift of Leadership.

Part I - The Challenge

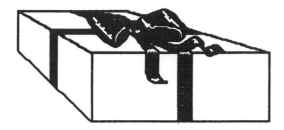

Chapter 1 - Understanding the Gift

A Guy Named Joe

Joe was one of the nicest people you'd ever want to meet. He was from a small town and had come from a hardworking, middle class family. When he was young he worked various construction jobs, and took a real liking to the electrical trade. He decided that he might make a career in construction, so he went through the training program and became a skilled professional.

Joe worked hard and made a good living, but he always knew that his dream was to eventually own his own business. After all, he thought, I'm a good technician. I work hard, I'm not afraid to take a chance, and I'm just as smart as the guy I work for. The only thing he had going for him, Joe thought, is that he put up some money and started his business. I can do the same.

So, he did. Joe took the risk, started his company, and became a successful electrical contractor. Along the way, he got involved in an electrical contractors' trade association and found that he enjoyed many of the aspects of working in a volunteer organization. He worked his way up through the leadership chairs at the local level, became a local chapter President, and then went through the same process at the state level. He thought he'd reached the peak when he became state President. But there was more to come.

Joe's organization decided they needed to affiliate with a national group, so they joined with a number of other contractor organizations to form a new federation of state and local groups. It was natural for Joe's state group to choose him to represent them in the formation of the new group. It was also natural for Joe to take on a leadership role, starting as the new national organization's Second Vice President. Joe put in his time for two years as Second VP, and was looking forward to the next steps: First Vice President (and President-elect), and then, in two more years, National President.

There was going to be just one small hitch in Joe's plan - he wasn't going to be nominated for higher office. The Chair of the Nominating Committee had been given the task of telling Joe that they (the Nominating Committee) just weren't comfortable putting him in line for the National Presidency. As much as the Chair and his Committee liked Joe, and appreciated his contributions to the organization, Joe had one shortcoming that they felt was too great. He was a terrible speaker.

Joe was terrified of large audiences, spoke too fast, had a thick regional accent, and a slight speech impediment. In a small group he was fine - he could handle a staff, was passable running a Committee meeting, and one-on-one his speech problems were overshadowed by his commitment and honesty. But being the President of a growing national association meant talking to audiences in the hundreds, perhaps thousands, addressing meetings of members and potential members all across the country, testifying in front of Congressional committees, and perhaps most importantly, working with the media wherever possible. The organization faced a big dilemma. If they didn't nominate Joe, they faced a

MAJOR internal problem. They even envisioned a floor fight at the Annual Meeting, something their reputation could not afford. If they did nominate Joe, they might spend two years worrying about his performance.

Someone had to tell Joe he wasn't going to be nominated, yet no one wanted to approach Joe and tell him it was his speaking ability (or rather his lack of ability) that stood in his way. To tell him that he had to take speaker's training would single him out. The association's leaders made an important decision that solved this particular problem, and had an even greater impact on Joe than the organization could have imagined.

The solution was actually pretty simple. Instead of sending Joe to training, they decided to adopt a policy that would require **all** National Officers to take speaker's training each year. This way, they didn't single out Joe and they assured that any future President would have been through at least 2-3 training courses before assuming the Presidency.

Joe was nominated and elected, and moved on to become National President. During his Presidency he was instrumental in helping the organization attain many of its goals. Was he ever a good speaker? Not really. Was he better than before taking the training sessions? Absolutely. He was certainly credible enough to carry out his years as President, but there was a lot more to it than just being a passable speaker.

On the last night of his Presidency, Joe gave what many thought was the best presentation of his life. His friends were proud, his doubters were impressed, and the organization was better off. It was Joe's wife, however, who described what had really happened to Joe because of his experience.

"Last Sunday was one of the happiest days of our lives," she said fighting back the tears. "Joe volunteered to do the reading at church. That's the first time he ever had the courage to get up in front of the congregation. There's no way he would ever have done that if he hadn't gained so much confidence and training from the association."

Joe had been given "The Gift".

Mel on the Brink

For most of his life, Mel had lived a pretty average existence. He had worked his way up in a major manufacturing company from mail room clerk to a secure, senior position in management. He married his hometown sweetheart, helped raise three children, enjoyed watching his kids play sports, and appeared to most of his friends and co-workers to be a regular guy. What a lot of people didn't know was that Mel was an alcoholic.

Mel's problems started like many addictions. It was "social" drinking with the neighbors, then those business dinners, and eventually stopping off after work for a few with the guys from the office. When Mel started drinking at lunch time, his supervisor finally took him aside and confronted him. Mel, of course, told him there was "no problem." In fact, there wasn't much problem at work, but the problems at home got worse and worse. Many nights Mel got so drunk they had to call his wife to come and get him. His kids, now grown and living away, didn't know how bad things were getting.

The real crisis for Mel started when they closed down his department and moved the company's operations to the west coast. Mel, at age 60, wasn't invited to go. He was offered "early retirement". The benefits were good - Mel wouldn't have to worry about money. He did have to worry about how he was going to pass the time every day, and how he was going to keep his self-respect after being told he wasn't needed anymore. Mel did what was probably the one thing a person in his situation shouldn't do - he drank even more. One Saturday night it wasn't the bar that called his wife, it was the police. Mel had hit bottom. His wife kicked him out of the house, he spent his days sitting around a hotel lobby, and he was finally ready to turn himself around.

Mel went back (for his third time) to Alcoholics Anonymous. With counseling and support, he improved his attitude and will power, and his wife took him back. With all this, Mel still felt empty. He was sober for the first time in years, he had financial security, and he had overcome a major life-threatening crisis, but he hadn't regained that day-to-day purpose that he had had when he was working for his firm for over 30 years. One day the local AA chapter office manager announced she was moving to Florida to retire with her husband. They needed a new office manager, and she asked Mel if he would be interested. It didn't pay anything, of course, but maybe he'd like to try it for a short time.

Mel was shocked. Why him, he wondered? Sure, he liked AA and what it did for people but he had never run a volunteer organization. What he had, he was told, was years of experience managing people, a track record of being an effective team player, and responsibility for multi-million dollar budgets. What else could the group want?

Mel talked to his wife, who immediately encouraged him to give it a shot. At first, Mel was really nervous. He had to gain the trust of the people who had been used to working with the previous manager. He was now the person who got the calls when someone had a problem. He had to open the office in the morning and he had to communicate with the state and national headquarters. On top of all this he still had to try to maintain his own sobriety. Mel was challenged in ways he wasn't used to being challenged.

As the days and weeks wore on, he got more and more comfortable in his new job. He began to realize that he could, in fact, use his business skills to run the local nonprofit AA group. Each day, he regained more and more of his old self respect. He knew that he was making a difference in people's lives and that made him feel good. Perhaps most important was the fact that he was back to having a real purpose when he woke up every day. He felt a true sense of accomplishment as the chapter grew and his work as manager led to more people getting help, the organization gaining financial stability, and Mel making a lot of new friends.

There was one more thing about Mel's role as a volunteer leader that he hadn't even noticed until one of his former coworkers from the company started participating in AA activities. The friend mentioned to Mel how smoothly the meetings were run, even though when they worked together Mel had never been responsible for any meetings or functions. He also commented on what a great job of fund raising Mel had done, but in his job Mel had never been in sales or marketing at all. Finally, Mel's friend told him, he had always thought that Mel hated being an organizer, that he always wanted to just go about his business and not be the center of attention, yet here he was acting like a ringmaster and seeming to enjoy it. What was the story, he wondered?

The story was that Mel had been given The Gift.

On the Job Experience

Jill graduated with honors in engineering and went to work for a research firm. She was not only intelligent and a hard worker, she was well liked by all of her co-workers. She seemed to have all of the tools to move ahead in her career, but she didn't have any real managerial experience.

Jill's manager wanted to give her a chance but there wasn't any position in the company that was right for someone with no experience. It was the old "catch-22" - she couldn't move ahead without experience and there was no way to get the experience. Her boss had a suggestion.

He felt that Jill should try to gain some experience by getting involved in a volunteer organization. He had been active in a local charity years earlier and knew they still needed volunteer leaders to help raise money and promote the group's work. He asked Jill to think about it.

Jill was like many young professionals and already had plenty of ways to fill up her "spare" time. In addition to her job, she was married and had a small child. She also liked to garden, read, and go bike riding. She wasn't sure she had the time to take on a volunteer role but she realized that in addition to giving her some experience, she might actually like the chance to make a difference in the lives of others. She decided to give it a try.

Jill was willing to help in any way she could and the group had plenty of work for her. She really enjoyed the organization and believed in the good work it was doing in the community. Within a couple of years she had worked her way up the organization's Board of Directors. As she moved up through the ranks of leadership, she gained experience that she would never have received in her role as a staff engineer.

One of her tasks as a Board member was to help with the group's fund raising efforts. She was asked to go out into the community and make presentations to the largest employers in the area. She also had to organize a fund raising campaign and chair several committees. All of these activities were new to Jill, and while they did require a lot of time, they also gave her a lot of confidence and experience.

The shy young engineer had become a salesperson, and a very good one.

Whether it was by design or by accident, Jill's employer had given her The Gift.

All of these people came from different backgrounds, different places and different situations, but there is a common thread among them. They all faced new challenges with an inherent set of values and skills that did not necessarily match up with these challenges. In most cases, people like Joe and Mel and Jill are thrown into situations and asked to "do the best you can". Their natural reaction is to draw on what they know and what they feel comfortable doing. Therein lies the key to their future and to the difference between "doing their best" and really having some impact. Good people with good intentions should be able to get things done. The problem isn't getting them to face the challenges of leadership, it's giving them a better chance to overcome the challenges. It's both a dilemma and an opportunity facing volunteer organizations and other institutions around the world. To make the greatest impact on the publics that organizations serve - members, donors, supporters, program recipients, etc.- these organizations need to understand - and give - the Gift. The Gift of Leadership is a simple concept.

The Gift of Leadership
is
What You Take Away
- and Use -
From Your Leadership Experience

In the case of Joe, the Gift wasn't just the ability to make better presentations or to better represent his organization, although those are certainly wonderful gifts. Joe's gifts included the self-confidence he gained, the satisfaction of having overcome a shortcoming, and the ability to touch other people's lives through his church.

Mel's gifts were just as obvious. His eventual success as an administrator proved to him that he could overcome challenges without a drink. He found that his newly-acquired skills as a meeting planner and fund raiser helped him in other situations, such as working with his homeowners' association.

Jill did take the gifts of leadership back to the lab, and the office, and they did help her become a more valued employee. Of greater value to Jill were the gifts she took to her family - the gifts of composure, and compromise, and confidence.

These volunteers, and millions like them, took the first step toward improving themselves and their organization by stepping forward and accepting a leadership role. They know (or learn) that in return for their volunteer input they will have a chance to contribute to a worthwhile cause and gain some level of recognition for their work. Certainly there is nothing wrong with using a feeling of contribution as a payback, and recognition is the best way to say thank you. But there is a limit to how much any person, or group of people, will give to a volunteer organization for the good feeling or recognition they get.

To truly take advantage of the opportunities that exist throughout the world to make this planet a better place for all, we need to make sure the volunteer spirit doesn't fade away with the constant call for volunteers to give more and more of themselves. Yes, there is a need for these volunteers, but these volunteers themselves have needs, too. If we make the Gift of Leadership a reality - even a goal - we can not only harness the resources of these volunteers we can actually increase the effectiveness of their efforts.

Giving volunteers the Gift of Leadership is one of the least understood yet most effective ways to reward volunteer leaders. The problem has been that volunteers have always had to gain the Gift by accident. In the future, with so much competition for the time and energy of volunteers, the organizations that will attract and keep the highest caliber leaders will be those which give the Gift by design, not by accident.

Chapter 2 - The Need to Serve

Volunteer organizations and institutions have existed for centuries, as has the need for people to volunteer to lead these organizations. In the United States, these organizations predate the nation itself. For example, the New York Chamber of Commerce was founded in 1768, and the American Philosophical Society in 1754 (with Benjamin Franklin as its first President). Sometimes they are formed and operate out of necessity - there is no one else to do the work. Many times these groups are centered around a specific cause or purpose, other times they are created out of a general belief that there are things that need to be changed. Historically, the basis for recruiting volunteers to lead these organizations has been a combination of appealing to a person's sense of commitment to whatever the cause or purpose of the organization is, and outright begging. In either case, the appeal to the volunteer has been one of give, give, give. Give your time, give your energy, give your knowledge, give your resources, give your money.

Part of the reason that people get "burned out" in volunteer organizations is this constant battle of getting others to take on leadership roles. The frustration of being turned down by others can build up on volunteer leaders and affect their own attitude toward the organization. The problem dosen't always lie with the people who won't give up their time. The problem often is that the person doing the asking (the volunteer) is too close to the situation. Because he/she is already committed to the organization, and knows the importance of being "involved", there is a frustration with others who don't believe as strongly. The hard thing to accept is that they are talking to "non-believers".

It's not that people don't believe in the work of the organization, they just don't believe that they have the time or commitment to volunteer to take on a leadership role. Take the situation of Michelle.

Michelle worked as a program director for a local social service organization. She had spent the last six years working with volunteer leaders from all walks of life. She believed she understood how volunteers felt about their organizations because she would often talk to her volunteer leaders about why they participated in her organization. Their reasons usually centered around the fact that they really believed in the work of the group and how it would help their community and the people in it. They mentioned some of the specific programs of the organization, such as the training programs and the fund raising for various charities and institutions. Michelle certainly understood their passion for the organization, since she worked there every day. She was convinced that if you find people who truly believe in the good work of an organization, you can attract volunteers to help out. Then she a got chance to find out that people who support an organization's purpose don't necessarily volunteer to help run it.

While driving home from work one afternoon, Michelle heard a radio announcement about a class reunion for a local high school. It reminded her that her class should be planning for their 20th reunion, and she wondered why she hadn't heard anything about it. When she got home she called her old high school and asked if anyone had contacted the school about running the reunion. No, she was told by the registrar, but there was a growing file of people from her class who had called to leave their names and addresses for whoever was running the reunion. Would Michelle be interested, she was asked?

Michelle gave it some thought. What the heck, she said to herself. It seemed like a simple enough task, and one that should be fun, too. Besides, the last reunion the class had - the 10-year reunion- hadn't really been very good, in her opinion. It was very unorganized, and didn't have a lot of creativity to it. Michelle was involved with putting on meetings all the time with her job and she felt that she could handle all of the logistical challenges pretty easily. On top of that, she had stayed in touch with a number of her friends from high school, and she knew she could count on them to help out. Building leadership teams of volunteers was another part of her job that she could transfer to the class reunion. Confident of her ability to run a first-rate reunion, she boldly told the school registrar to send her the file, and to put her down as the Chairperson for the class reunion.

After getting the file from the school, Michelle decided that the first thing she needed to do was exactly what they would do at her work - she needed to form a committee. She decided to start with a few of the people who had worked on the previous reunion. She called the Chairperson from that group and asked if she would like to help out again for the 20th.

"No way," was the immediate response. "I'm still recovering from the last one. I've got about four boxes of stuff left over from that reunion down in my basement. You're welcome to them."

Michelle had received her first rejection, and had been given a first-hand look at the results of volunteer burnout. It wouldn't be her last, either. There were several other turndowns before she got her committee together and began planning the reunion. Although things turned out fine, and the reunion was a big success, Michelle could never understand why some people came forward and were eager to help while others wanted nothing to do with the reunion work.

It's a good question, Michelle.

The need to volunteer and seek a leadership role can't be defined in one general statement, as it is most certainly an individual need. Some people volunteer out of instinctual goodness, some do it out of religious or moral conviction, and others volunteer to promote a personal need or belief. Some people, however, volunteer to get something out of their leadership experience that they don't get in other parts of their lives.

There are those who may be at the bottom of the organizational chart in their companies but are at the top of the organizational chart in their volunteer role in their church, civic or business organization, or professional society. Others have more friends at their volunteer organization than they have at home or at work. Still others get more respect and attention from their peers at a voluntary organization than anywhere else in their private or professional lives. Organizations have a great opportunity to get the most from these people if they (the organizations) can get beyond the constant "give".

To do that, there is a need to stop looking at leadership from a believer's viewpoint and look at it from the nonbeliever's viewpoint. Like it or not, the nonbeliever wants to know what's in it (the leadership role) for her/him, not just what's in it for the organization.

The main reason people give for NOT wanting to serve is that they don't have the time. They are already committed with family, jobs, hobbies, etc., and really can't see how they could possibly find any more time to devote to a leadership role in a voluntary organization. Surely, these people ARE busy, but they also have the same 24 hour day that everyone else has. SOMEONE is doing this important volunteer work, why can't they?

It isn't that they don't have the time, it's just that they don't see how this volunteer role is more important than what they're already doing. Getting past that barrier is crucial to getting people to volunteer and take that first step toward the Gift.

One of the answers to the "Why should I volunteer?" question may lie in a book written several years ago by Dick Huseman and John Hatfield. The book is entitled *And After All I've Done*. The authors wrote this book under the premise that as people go through various relationships in their lives (i.e. husband-wife relationships, parent-child relationships, employer-employee relationships, etc.) they constantly keep two mental lists about the various relationships. These lists consist of 1) What am I putting into this relationship? and 2) What am I getting out of this relationship? When these lists get out of balance - when people perceive that they are putting more into a relationship than they are getting out of it - they have two choices: they can get "even" or they can get out.

According to the studies conducted by Huseman and Hatfield, tens of thousands of people quit their jobs every day, even in the poorest of economic times. When asked about this - about how they could quit a job in times of economic uncertainty -

the responses fell into many categories. When these answers are analyzed, however, they seem to point toward a single "underlying" feeling. "After all I've done for this employer, this is all I have to show for it, and it's not worth it anymore."

Hatfield and Huseman took their relationship theory into the workplace, and asked employees what they wanted from their employer. What made it worth coming into work another day rather than quitting and going to work for someone else? The results of this part of their study were very interesting. The respondents (all salaried employees, working for other people) listed a number of things they looked for from their employer. These included:

- Doing challenging work
- A feeling of achievement
- Pay
- Job security
- A sense of accomplishment
- Fringe benefits
- Promotion and advancement
- Recognition for good work

and several others.

Of those that showed up on the list, the three most frequently given answers were:

1) A sense of accomplishment
2) Recognition for good work
3) Pay

What these people seem to be saying is that their job title or job description isn't so important. What's most important is that they get a feeling that they are doing something worthwhile- that they are accomplishing something. Also, if they are working at a worthwhile job and doing it well (accomplishing something) they expect someone besides themselves to acknowledge the fact that they are making a contribution (recognition for good work). Finally, in the workplace, if someone is doing a good job at something worthwhile and the employer wants to show that he/she recognizes that contribution, there is an easy and obvious way to express appreciation (pay).

While Huseman and Hatfield didn't have voluntary organizations in mind when they wrote their book, their findings are just as applicable in the volunteer world. When you ask people to take on a leadership role in a volunteer organization, aren't you asking them to go to work for the organization? In fact, when asking people to volunteer, most of the time we actually say "We'd like you to do some WORK for the organization", or 'There's a JOB we'd like you to take on." If being a volunteer leader means going to work, it seems logical that people in this volunteer work force want the same things everyone else does from their work.

What does this mean to volunteer organizations? It means that in order to manage this volunteer work force, you need to use the most desired motivators - a sense of accomplishment, recognition for good work, and ....PAY? Unfortunately, in volunteer organizations one of the most important motivators - pay- isn't available to leaders. If the number three motivator isn't an option, that means that numbers one and two - accomplishment and recognition - are even more important.

In the case of volunteer leaders the number one concern is certainly time, but it's not spent time that concerns people, it's *wasted* time. What these busy people are telling organizations is: "If I'm going to give up my valuable time to go to work for your organization, you had better make sure that you ask me to do something worthwhile. And, if I do that, if I give up my time and try my very best to accomplish something, I expect someone to say 'thank you, thank you, thank you."

In the case of motivating volunteer leaders, these two outcomes are critical. Give them a worthwhile job, and then give them the recognition they deserve. In fact, in volunteer organizations, number two (recognition) actually becomes two AND three (pay) because the recognition that is given becomes the volunteer's paycheck. No matter what "job" people have, if they stop getting paid they will eventually stop coming to work. Getting others to serve in leadership roles means understanding the need to serve, and understanding what they expect in return for their service.

Chapter 3 - The Big Picture

Voluntary organizations always seem to be focused on a mission, or a vision. Certainly all institutions and organizations should know what they are trying to accomplish, and who they are trying to serve (society, members, the disadvantaged, etc.). There is an even deeper purpose to volunteer organizations that needs to be examined. This purpose goes beyond any specific constituency and to the very core of why ANY of these groups exist.

It might seem as though there are already more than enough institutions or organizations to serve any need that could possibly exist. There isn't a person or thing that you come into contact with on a daily basis that doesn't have some organization claiming to represent them. In democracies like the United States, most of our daily needs are supposedly represented by some branch of our government. We have the legislative branch to represent our views, we have the executive branch to carry out the laws, to protect our possessions and to provide us with safety, and we have the judiciary to protect our rights under the laws. We seem to have all of our needs covered, right?

Not necessarily. Voluntary organizations fill a void that exists even in the most democratic and open systems. All people cherish personal freedoms, yet those freedoms don't always assure people that they are being heard by those who matter the most. The concept of one person, one vote is a wonderful and valuable concept, and one that has been the cornerstone of much of what is held dear in free societies. Still, that doesn't mean that the system always works the way it should.

The "mission" of voluntary groups should actually be secondary to the purpose of those groups. Authors and politicians and great thinkers have been trying for years to come up with a definition that states clearly and effectively what these volunteer groups are supposed to be doing. Perhaps the best description of the "purpose" of voluntary organizations can be summed up in four words:

"TO GIVE VOICE TO..........."

No other definition sums it up so concisely. That's exactly what volunteer organizations are supposed to do. This is by no means limited to membership organizations or "special interest groups". The term "to give voice to" applies to virtually any voluntary organization. It's not about having the RIGHT to be heard, it's about having the ABILITY to be heard. One social worker can express his or her opinions about ways to make day-to-day life better for certain individuals or groups within a society, but hundreds of thousands of social workers speaking with one "voice" can actually change the conditions under which those people or groups live. One volunteer can reach out and teach others how to improve their lives, but thousands of volunteers united through an institution or organization can literally create a better life for others. One engineer (the so-called special interest group) can talk about the need to study safety factors associated with some new technology, while tens of thousands of engineers, working together through their volunteer organization, can establish standards that will save lives around the world.

This concept of "to give voice to" goes far beyond accomplishing a specific group's goals. A good example of what voluntary organizations can mean to a society is what is happening in the "new" South Africa. When Nelson Mandela announced that he would not seek an additional term as President, there was great concern around the world about the country's ability to sustain the march toward a truly open and free society. After all, it was reasoned, so much of what had been accomplished was directly attributable to Mandela's charisma and forcefulness that there was certainly no one who could fill his shoes and continue to lead at the same level. That was what most outside of South Africa believed. Inside South Africa, there were others who felt differently.

"Certainly, Mandela is a very large pebble on the beach," said Archbishop Desmond Tutu, "but he is still only one pebble. There are many others. We are establishing institutions here in South Africa that will have the ability to sustain themselves without having to depend upon any one individual. It will be these institutions, not the individuals, that will determine how far our nation will go."

The institutions to which Tutu referred included the nation's new constitution and government, the new economic systems, and certainly the new push for individual freedoms. Another institution on which South Africa is counting is the institution of voluntary organizations. These organizations have several purposes in the new South Africa.

First of all, they will assure that the newly enfranchised black community will indeed be heard. Voluntary organizations will "give voice to" many of the individuals and businesses who have no other method of expressing their individual and collective views. Secondly, the changes in South Africa don't assure the success of anyone, they only assure equal *opportunity to be successful.* Some entity will have to train the emerging groups how to be successful in this new, open society. The South African government certainly doesn't have the resources to do it all on its own, but by encouraging the establishment of voluntary organizations the government can assist the people in helping themselves.

Finally, voluntary organizations have the ability to go beyond the training of people in various trades and professions. Through *leadership* in these voluntary organizations South Africans are acquiring skills that will help them lead not only their organizations but also, in the very near future, the country itself.

If there is any doubt about the value of leadership in voluntary organizations, one need look no further than the political, business, and social leaders in the United States. Almost universally, these people have honed their skills and abilities in the leadership ranks of America's non-profit, volunteer organizations.

Virtually all business leaders have been active in trade or professional organizations in a volunteer leadership role. In most cases, they have been active in leadership in several organizations and have drawn on their experiences in all of these groups. The automobile company executive who served as an officer in a manufacturing trade association is just as likely to have also been a leader in a Scouting organization or a homeowners' association. It's also just as likely that the skills and experience gained through the Scouting organization were just as valuable in the business world as the experience that came with involvement in the trade association. Is it just a coincidence that ALL of these business leaders were active in volunteer leadership roles? If being in that volunteer leadership position wasn't important, why would all of these people be so insistent that their leadership roles be included in their resumes and introductions? They realize that this type of experience adds to their credibility as industry leaders.

The politician with no voluntary leadership background would be hard-pressed to be elected in many cases. This type of involvement, whether in a legal society, a trade group, a service club, or a charity, is part of what people look for in a candidate to establish leadership credibility. Do any of these politicians take on a volunteer leadership role to help their political careers? Absolutely! So what? As was mentioned before, there are many reasons people seek leadership roles. We'd like to believe that there wouldn't be such a "greedy" motive for serving but it really doesn't matter. Most of these people are talented individuals who assist the organization in achieving its goals, so everyone gains. What is more probably true is the fact that these politically-motivated people gain much more than a line on a resume when they assume voluntary leadership roles. They gain real insight into the importance of volunteer organizations, and understand why people need these groups to be heard. They also gain the Gift of Leadership, and that will help them be more effective in representing their constituencies in the future.

The field of social issues and social service is where voluntary organizations have done the most to "give voice to" those who would otherwise go unheard. Leaders in these organizations have an additional advantage - and an additional challenge - in the passion that people have for their causes or programs. The ability to harness this passion is another skill that leaders in these organizations must have, or gain, to take full advantage of the strong beliefs of their members or supporters.

On the other hand, this passion also can cause great rifts within the organization. The ability to negotiate with those whose passionate ideas and beliefs are in conflict is one of the greatest skills that a leader can possess. In mastering this skill, leaders can often use that skill to make the organization's voice heard by more people and institutions than those organizations who tend to be always in agreement. It's no wonder that the leaders of these groups often possess excellent communication and negotiating skills when they represent their organizations in public. They've honed these skills within their organization. They've gained the Gift, and they've used that Gift to further their causes or programs.

These are among the reasons why voluntary organizations and the leaders who serve them have been so important to the institution of democracy, and why they are so important to the future. To give the Gift, voluntary organizations need to understand its impact and be organized to deliver it.

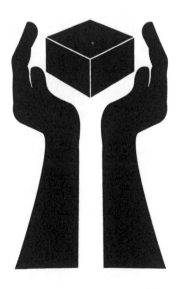

Part II - Creating Successful Volunteers

Chapter 4 - The Need to Succeed

Hal was really excited about his new assignment. It wasn't because he was going to make any more money. In fact, he wasn't going to make ANY money at all. His new assignment wasn't at work, where he knew his skill as an accountant could always meet the challenge. This assignment was different because he was taking on a completely new challenge as the Chair of the Annual Fundraising Committee for his son's Scout troop.

He had always taken pride in his ability to work with clients and handle their accounting needs. He was even more proud of his son, Steve, who worked hard at school and was basically a good kid. Hal worried about Steve when he was very young, because he wasn't into sports like all of his friends. When Steve discovered Scouting, he really grew as a person. That's why Hal was so willing to take on a leadership role as Fundraising Chair. He wanted to give something back to the troop that had given so much confidence and enjoyment to his son. It made sense, after all - an accountant involved with money.

Hal wasn't a "salesman", but he had seen a couple of the Fundraising Chairs before him operate, and he was sure he could handle the job. Besides, here was a chance for him to shine as something other than a staff accountant at his firm. He also had some great ideas on fundraising that he wanted to try out.

Despite his enthusiasm and desire to help, Hal's experience as Fundraising Chair wasn't what he thought it was going to be. When he asked the troop leader what his goal was, the leader said "Raise as much money as you can." When Hal wanted to get some more detail on exactly what he needed to do, he was told to talk to last year's chair. Unfortunately for Hal, last year's chair (and his son) had moved out of town. What Hal had to start with were some records in a file box but not in any particular order. Nevertheless, Hal was confident and determined when he started to assemble his committee.

His first stumbling block was trying to convince some of the other parents to work with him. "Fundraising?" many replied. "I'm not going to hit up all my friends and neighbors for money. I'll do something else - maybe drive to one of the campouts or keep the membership records."

Finally, Hal managed to get four other parents to agree to serve on his committee. Now, he thought, we can finally get some things done. He scheduled his first committee meeting and was ready to start. Hal spent several hours drawing up a plan of action, complete with assignments for each committee member, goals for each person, and a time line for completion of each task. At the meeting, Hal presented his plan and asked if any of the others had any other ideas. To Hal's surprise, there wasn't much discussion. Hal guessed that the others must have really liked his plan.

As the fundraising efforts started, Hal's frustration level grew. None of the other committee members seemed to be available to do the work, so Hal found himself trying to do more and more of it. On top of that, fundraising was a lot harder than Hal thought it was going to be. The people and companies he expected to be his primary sources of money were reluctant to write checks. They all seemed to have questions that Hal wasn't sure how to answer. He figured that it was easy to explain why it was important to give money to scouting but not everyone saw it that way. Things weren't going very well, and Hal sure wasn't having any fun. At his next committee meeting, only two others even showed up.

Hal stayed with the job and did the best he could. Toward the end of the program year, the Scoutmaster and a couple of the other troop leaders took Hal aside and asked if he would be willing to let them help out, since fundraising was well below last year. Hal agreed, then had to stand aside while the others took over his program.

Despite the setbacks, the troop managed to raise enough money to do what they wanted to do. At the big Troop Banquet at the end of the year they even gave Hal a nice plaque. He appreciated the plaque but felt pretty bad about the way things had gone during the year. When a sheet came around to all of the scout parents during the summer, asking for volunteers to work on committees next year, Hal decided not to sign up. His career as a volunteer leader was over.

What went wrong for Hal? It seemed as though this was going to be another of those success stories that fill the history of many volunteer organizations, another of those stories about someone receiving the Gift and moving ahead with his or her life. Hal appeared to have what it takes to be an effective leader - a good attitude, a plan of action, enthusiasm, etc. Yet Hal had the one thing you never want a volunteer to have - a bad experience. Could anything have made this a good experience for Hal instead of a bad one?

Not only *could* this have been a good experience for Hal, it *should* have been. One of the overriding goals of any volunteer structure should be to create successful volunteers. The word "create" may conjure up images of some sort of

Frankenstein monster but that's not the case. Creating successful volunteers actually means taking the volunteer's innate need to serve and adding to it the Gift of Leadership.

It was noted earlier that the number one need of anyone "working" for a volunteer organization is a sense of accomplishment. Hal got off to a bad start when he was told to "raise as much money as you can". How was Hal to know when he had accomplished anything if he didn't know what was expected?

The second most important need of volunteers is the need to receive recognition for good work. The scout troop tried to provide this to Hal by giving him a plaque at the big awards program, but Hal - and most of the other troop leaders - knew that Hal really didn't earn the award. So instead of getting the two things he wanted for working for the troop, Hal now had neither.

When people tell us that they want a sense of accomplishment in their work they are also saying that they want to be *successful*. It doesn't matter if it's a paying job or a volunteer job, no one wants to be a failure. In many volunteer organizations, leaders are successful in spite of the obstacles they face. That's if the organization and the individual are lucky and everything works out o.k. Wouldn't it make a lot more sense to put a program in place that will raise the chances that volunteers **will** be successful, rather than depending upon luck to make it happen?

"Motivating" workers in any environment - volunteer or paid - is one of the hardest parts of leadership. There are basically two ways to really motivate people: 1) through fear and 2) by instilling self-confidence. Using fear often works in the short run, but is normally a disaster in the long run. People who work with a constant fear of failure are certainly motivated, but that's a difficult way to run a business. It's an <u>impossible</u> way to run a volunteer organization. Positive motivation in a work force comes when people have confidence in themselves, in the skills they possess, and in their ability to communicate and get along with others.

Motivation and success go together. If organizations are going to reignite and harness the power of volunteers in the future, they are going to have to learn how to create successful volunteers. To do that they really need a plan, not a prayer. A systematic approach to creating successful volunteer leaders entails five steps:
1) Recruiting the "right" people the right way
2) Orienting new leaders
3) Giving the Gift
4) Getting something done (accomplishing something)
5) Delivering the paycheck

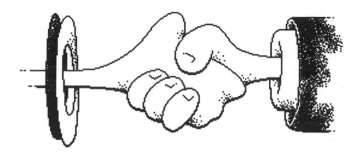

Chapter 5 - Recruiting the Right Volunteers the Right Way

Donna was so glad to be the new President of her Society she could hardly stand it. After all the years of serving on committees and then the Board, she had been elected as Secretary six long years ago. Then she waited until it was her "turn". Two years as Secretary, two years as Treasurer, two years as Vice President. Finally, her time had come to be President and she wasn't going to waste any time getting started. As President, she wanted to make her mark on the Society's educational efforts, and she hoped to be remembered for those efforts in the Society's history.

Donna called the Society's Executive Director and said she was ready to get together and begin getting her leadership team in place for the new program year. The Executive Director had been with the Society for nearly eight years, and had done a superb job. During her tenure as Executive Director the Society had grown each year, there had been increased recognition of the group's certification and designation programs and the conferences and meetings continued to attract larger and larger audiences. Yes indeed, Donna thought, our Executive Director is one of the best.

Donna and the Executive Director sat down and began discussing where to start on the list of potential Committee Chairs for the new year. Donna looked down the list of Committees, and it was a little frightening.

Education	Government Relations
Nominating	Annual Meeting
Finance	Membership
Accreditation	Editorial

Eight committees to fill. She decided to start with the easiest one - Membership.

The Executive Director asked Donna if she had anyone in mind for Membership Chair. "I think I'm going to ask Barbara," she replied. "She and I worked together on some fundraising for our college alumni group a few years ago. Plus, she owes me a favor from a project we worked on together for our office." Donna picked up the phone and called Barbara at work.

"Barbara, hi. This is Donna. How are things going?"

"Oh, you know. The usual," Barbara replied. "Between the kids and work, there's always too much to do and not enough time for anything. What's up?"

"Well," Donna continued, "as you know, I'm going to be President of our Society this year. I'm down here right now at our Society headquarters with our Executive Director. My first job as President is to appoint the new Committee Chairs and we're doing a lot of that work today. In fact, we've been going through all of the committees and we're down to the Membership Committee, and you'll never guess whose name just came up!"

After a long silence, Barbara finally replied. "Look, Donna, is this the kind of thing that's going to take a lot of time, 'cause I'm really swamped right now?"

"Nah," said Donna. "Membership is kind of *everybody's* job. Besides, we're going to have this 'member-get-a-member' campaign this year that's going to be just dynamite. Do you know the best thing about being membership chair in our Society? Our Executive Director. Ever since she's been here membership has been going great. She does a wonderful job. But Barb, you kinda know what membership is all about. After all, we worked on that alumni fundraiser. What do you say?"

Barbara again hesitated before responding. "Donna, I don't know. Is this one of those jobs where I have to get up in front of the members and give a report? I hate to do any kind of public presentations, you know."

The words had hardly left Barbara's mouth when Donna shot back. "Naw! You see, Barbara, every month our Executive Director puts together a membership report for the Board. After all, she's the one who works with the numbers every day. But really, Barb, I've got eight committees I've got to find chair people for. I sure need someone to take this membership job. What do you say?"

Barbara tried again. "Look, Donna. Is this membership deal one of those situations where if I don't get enough members the Society is going to have money problems? I sure don't want that kind of pressure."

"Barb - you're not listening!" came Donna's retort. "It's like I said - membership is kind of *everybody's* job. And I just know that this member-get-a-member program is going to be great.

Anyway, our Executive Director does SUCH a good job with membership. What do you say?"

Finally, Barbara sighed, "I'll tell you what. Why don't you make a few more calls. If you can't find someone else, give me a call back."

Donna turned to the Executive Director and said, "Sign up Barbara for Membership Chair. What's the next committee?"

This scenario might sound funny, or a little far-fetched, but thousands and thousands of volunteers are recruited this way every day. Some would say, "So what? She got the job filled by someone she knows. Everything will work out."

Maybe. If Barbara turns out to be a good, successful membership chair - and really feels that she *accomplished* something - it's probably going to be in spite of, rather than because of, the way she was recruited. There are two parts to the problem here. The first part is the way Barbara was selected as Donna's choice to chair the membership committee.

Donna, while certainly well-intentioned, is faced with a basic human fear - the fear of rejection. Since no one likes to be turned down, she decided to ask someone who had a high likelihood of saying yes. In many cases such as this, the "recruiter" (Donna) goes through the process of thinking of friends, other busy people, last year's chair, whose turn it is, etc., etc. That's how people like Barbara get on the list of candidates.

 Before determining who will take the job, before even thinking about any individual or candidate, Donna needs to take a step back and look at the job itself. What kind of person does the organization want for membership chair? What personal traits or characteristics does a good membership person have? Just as importantly, what skills does such a person possess that will enable him or her to be successful, and really accomplish something in this volunteer leadership role?

Over the past 15 years, tens of thousands of volunteer and staff leaders have participated in workshops on the topic of recruiting the right person for this membership chairperson's role. Although the specific responsibilities of the membership chair may vary slightly from group to group, there were some consistent answers to these questions about what kind of person makes a good membership chair, and what skills that person will need to be successful. The most frequently mentioned were:

CHARACTERISTICS	**SKILLS**
accessible	communications
believes in the organization's mission	delegation
	facilitation
flexible	listening
friendly	marketing
goal-oriented	negotiating
knowledgeable about the organization	planning
	speaking
outgoing	sales
persistent	time management
sense of humor	writing
successful	
visionary	

A wonderful list of characteristics and skills, to be sure. But what are the chances of finding anyone with ALL of these characteristics and ALL of these skills? Not much of a chance at all. That's not the point of the exercise. The point is that before Donna, or any leader, starts asking people to take on the membership job she should make a list like this one (at least mentally, if not in writing) and think about what the "perfect" membership chair would look like. Knowing that she's not going to find the perfect person, she can set her own priorities as to which of these characteristics and skills are most important and see who (if anyone) in her organization has some of the important qualities in both lists. Donna may find that she actually has more choices than she thinks, with each candidate having a number of important qualities.

For example, let's say that Barbara was selected not just because Donna thought she could get her to say "yes" but because she had a number of important characteristics (successful, persistent, knowledgeable about the organization, friendly, and a believer in the organization's mission). On the skill side, she is a good negotiator, an effective time manager, has some basic marketing skills, and writes a very nice business letter. Not bad to start with, is it? There may be other people with different combinations of characteristics and skills, but Barbara is actually a pretty good choice with a real chance to succeed. She's got so many positive characteristics that the fact that she isn't perfect doesn't matter. You do the best you can with characteristics because, after all, you can't change the kind of person she is.

The skills, on the other hand, are a different story. You *can* teach a person to be a better speaker or presenter, you *can* teach a person how to facilitate a good committee meeting, you *can* help a person learn how to be more effective at selling memberships. If Donna (and her organization) knows that Barbara would really do a great job, and be more successful as membership chair if she was just a little better at facilitating a meeting or overcoming objections, not only CAN the organization teach her to do those things, it actually has an OBLIGATION to help. The organization's job is to recruit good people and then give them the skills to be more successful than they would have been without the skill training. That, after all, IS the Gift of Leadership.

The other part of the problem entails not just who was asked to take the job, but how she was asked to take it. Donna's priority in this situation was to find someone who would say "yes" when asked to take the job. Donna wanted to fill that organization chart and move on with her goals as President. Barbara wants to do something worthwhile with her time.

These two objectives shouldn't be mutually exclusive. They should work together to create a good experience for the individuals and provide valuable help for the organization. However Barbara's name came up, that doesn't mean she won't be a good leader if she feels committed to the task. Unfortunately, she wasn't asked for any commitment.

Look back at how the conversation went between Donna and Barbara. Donna began by saying she was "down to the membership committee". Is this a great way to start building up Barbara's sense of accomplishment? It actually sounds as if all the good jobs were gone and membership is the only one left! Then Donna continues underselling the position by stating that it won't take much time, there won't be any pressure, and someone else (the Executive Director) will probably do most of the work anyway. Barbara is probably thinking, "If that's all there is to the job, why even bother having a volunteer do it - just do it yourself or let the staff director do it." She'd have every right to think that she was just going to be going through the motions and not really accomplishing anything.

What Donna should have done, despite her fear of rejection, is be honest and enthusiastic with Barbara. Enthusiastic to show how important the job is, and honest to make sure that Barbara is committed to giving it her best shot.

"Barbara, this is Donna. As you know I'm going to be President of our organization this year. One of my first jobs is to appoint our Committee Chairs for next year, and I'm down here today at the organization's headquarters with our Executive Director to do just that. We're starting with one of the most important jobs, Barb, the Membership Committee. We think you're the kind of person, with the skills we need, to do a great job in membership, and I'd like you to work with me this year to help the organization grow. What do you say?"

Barbara's concerns will still be the same.

"Is this going to take a lot of time?"

Donna needs to be honest. "Barb, there's no getting around it. If we're going to get more people to join the organization it's going to take some time and effort. We estimate about 3-4 hours a month, plus committee meetings 4 times a year. You'll have plenty of help, especially from our Executive Director. She's terrific in coordinating a lot of the membership activities but she needs a good volunteer leader to really make things happen. I think you're the right member for her to work with. What do you say?"

Barbara will probably come back with another objection.

"Is this one of those things where I have to get up in front of the group and give reports, because I don't like that kind of stuff?"

"Barb," Donna should reply, "we do ask you to report to the Board on a quarterly basis, so we can see where you might need some help. It's not a requirement to address the membership meetings unless you want to."

Barbara will still try one more time.

"Well, I'm not sure, Donna. Does this mean if we don't get enough new members the organization is going to be in financial trouble, because if that's the kind of pressure I'll be under I'm not sure I want to do it?"

"Barbara," Donna should say, "membership is probably our most important committee. That's EXACTLY why I'm asking you. You'll have the help of our Executive Director, and I'll certainly be willing to do what I can to make this membership program work, but I think your leadership can make this our best year ever. How about working with me to make our organization grow?"

If Barbara takes this job, at least she's committed to what the membership job really is, and not just doing it as a favor to Donna. In some ways, it's probably better for Barbara to turn down the second offer than to accept the first one. At least that way Donna knows that she needs to find another membership chair, rather than kidding herself by thinking that Barbara is out there working hard.

There is one aspect about Donna's recruitment of Barbara that WAS done correctly from the beginning. That was the fact that Donna - a volunteer - was the one who did the actual recruiting/asking. She could have let the Executive Director do that, either in person, on the phone, or through a letter. However, it is critical to the process of creating successful leaders that volunteers always recruit volunteers. This is important for three reasons:

    1) It shows that the volunteer leader is taking his or her responsibility seriously, and is willing to risk being rejected rather than delegating this important responsibility to staff.

2) It is important that the person being asked to take on a volunteer leadership role is asked by someone who is already making the same commitment of time and energy that is being asked of others.

3) Even in volunteer situations, it is sometimes necessary to discipline or even "fire" workers, and this can be done only by the person who "hired" them. Firing a volunteer is a job that should be done by another volunteer.

Does the organization's staff have any role in recruiting key volunteer leaders? Absolutely. The staff's role is to help the volunteer leader who will do the actual recruiting decide who the best candidates are. The staff person should help create, on a job by job basis, that list of desired characteristics and skills that the organization should be looking for in key leadership positions. After the list is created, the staff person should help identify those people within the organization who most closely match the list of desired qualities.

If an organization is going to create successful volunteers, it needs to get them off to the best possible start. To do that requires a "resource check" before starting to fill in an organization chart. Instead of "Who will take the job?" the first question should be "What are our choices?" Asking the right person the right way is the safest and most efficient way to start building a leadership team that can truly make an impact.

Chapter 6 - Management By Assumption

It was hard for Kevin to figure out why things had fallen through for his group. As President, he was sure he had done a good job of recruiting officers and committee chairs. What's more, after getting everyone to agree to take a leadership job, he sat down with the group's Executive Director and developed some pretty detailed job descriptions for everyone. He sent those out and even followed up with phone calls to each Board member and committee chair to ask if they had any questions. Nobody did. That didn't surprise Kevin too much, since most of the people on the Board had been around for a long time. Even the new people seemed to know what was expected of them, so what was Kevin supposed to do? These were mature people who certainly had the good sense to ask for help or clarification if they needed it, and no one asked.

Kevin started to realize that some things were off track when he called the Executive Director for an update on the plans for the Annual Meeting.

"I have no idea," replied the Executive Director. "I haven't heard from the Committee Chair yet. He was supposed to talk to the leaders and give me some dates to look at so I could start working with the hotels, but he hasn't called."

Kevin immediately called Bob, the Annual Meeting Chair.

"Dates? I thought the date was already set for December 4th," Bob said. "In fact, I already got a signed contract with the Elks Club. Since I'm a member we can get the hall for next to nothing. The only thing we can't do is serve any alcohol, since they lost their liquor license last year. Why didn't the Exec say anything to me about the date not being confirmed? I'll tell you something, Kevin, that Exec has been treading on some thin ice for a while. I hope he's not going to drop the ball on this Annual Meeting like he's been doing on that lawsuit we're fighting."

"Great," thought Kevin. "Another staff versus member situation. We've got the most talented group of volunteer leaders we've ever had and we seem to keep spinning our wheels on every little detail. I probably ought to sit down with the Exec again and find out what's going on with him and some of these members."

Kevin didn't need to worry about the situation for too long. The morning after the group's next Board Meeting, Kevin woke up to see this "horror headline" covering the front page in the state's largest newspaper.

He's Out: Exec Fired By Board

As bad as that looked, the article that followed was even worse.

Without explanation, the Executive Director of the ABC organization was fired last night in a divisive coup that one Board member labeled a "witch hunt". The Exec, who had been a member of the association prior to becoming it's Executive Director two years ago, was called into the group's Board meeting and told he was fired. "The only thing I was told," said the Exec, "was that I served at the pleasure of the Board and I no longer pleasured the Board."

Only eight of the 20 Board members attended the meeting, but two cast ballots for absentees. That made the vote against the Executive Director 6-4.

"The reputation of the group was hurt by its inability to run a smooth operation," said one Board member. "I'm bothered that a Board that proposes to be an advocate for fairness can act in such an inhumane and unprofessional manner."

"It's done as far as I'm concerned," said the Board's Vice President. "He disagreed with how things needed to be done."

That explanation surprised the Board's attorney, who told reporters that the issues involved predated the Executive Director's appointment to his job.

The Board's treasurer noted that the organization "needs to redouble its fundraising efforts."

Kevin read the article three times before convincing himself that it was real and not some terrible joke.

Welcome to management by assumption, Kevin.

What Kevin faced in these situations is not uncommon in volunteer organizations. In the case of Bob, his Annual

Meeting Chair, Bob assumed that as Chair he had the authority and responsibility to secure a meeting location and execute a contract on behalf of the group. The Executive Director assumed that the Chair wouldn't take any action until it was cleared through him. Kevin assumed that both of them would let him know what was going on and tell him if there were any problems.

The second situation was really a classic in the annals of management by assumption. The Executive Director assumed that if there was a problem with the way he was doing things, someone would sit down and talk to him before it reached the point that his job was in danger. The Board assumed they could conduct business with less than half the Board present and that the Board could fire the Exec if he didn't "pleasure" them any longer. Several leaders assumed that, as members of the Board, they were free to talk to the press about anything that happened within the organization.

When eight different leaders have eight different ideas about what each person is supposed to be doing within the organization, what you have is chaos. What you have is management by assumption.

Management by assumption usually refers to the situation where everyone assumes that everyone knows what to do, and no one wants to affront anyone's intelligence by asking a few simple questions such as "Do you understand what your job is and how it relates to everything else?" Why ask that kind of question when you told them what you expected when you recruited them and then gave them those written job descriptions? Why can't they just go to work and do what they agreed to do?

The reason it doesn't work that way is that the leaders may have been given specific tasks to do or projects to oversee, but no one explained how those tasks or projects fit into the bigger scheme of things within the organization. No one explained the resources available or the authority each leader had, and no one explained what the volunteer was supposed to be doing and what the staff was supposed to be doing.

Yet if proper recruitment is done, there should be a good chance of getting a good person to agree to take on a leadership role and really give it a good try. The written job description is certainly a good way to inform individuals what is expected of them. However, the work of volunteer organizations isn't done by individuals working alone, it is done by teams of individuals working together through Boards, committees, task forces, etc. One of the ways to cut down on the problems caused by management by assumption is to hold a leadership orientation.

Getting Everyone Going in the Same Direction

Most effective volunteer organizations have some sort of leadership orientation session each year. This sometimes takes the form of a "retreat" which could last one to two days. Other groups simply extend one of their scheduled leadership meetings and devote whatever time is necessary to the orientation process. In some cases, organizations believe that it's only the new leaders who need this orientation so they design it to inform only these new people.

In almost all cases, the annual leadership orientation should include ALL of the organization's key leaders. This would usually include the officers, Board members, and committee chairs. Some organizations also include their committee members in this process. There are several reasons why these leadership orientations are important:

1) It assures that all of the leaders are getting the same information at the same time and in the same manner. This eliminates the situation where one person or group hears the information from one individual and the next person or group hears it from someone else. Each presentation of the material is bound to be a little different, and that little difference often leads to management by assumption.

2) Newer leaders get to see that other busy people have made the same commitment to the organization that they are making. This is a great testimonial to the organization. When new leaders come to the orientation they are probably still a little unsure about whether or not they've made the right decision in agreeing to serve. When they see the current leaders at the orientation they realize that this organization must be worthwhile if all of these busy people are willing to give their valuable time to a leadership role.

3) Current leaders get to see the new leadership "in action" sooner. The leadership orientation is the first time that some of the new leaders are asked to participate at the top levels of the organization and that makes this a perfect time for current leaders to evaluate the new leaders and determine where they might need some help.

4) Relationships and responsibilities can be discussed. This is the most important part of the orientation because this is where the assumptions are confronted and cleared up. This can only be done if all of the key leaders participate in the orientation. Of special importance in this area is the relationship between volunteer leaders and the organization's staff (if it has one). Newer leaders have probably only dealt with the organization's staff on a program or project basis. As organizational leaders, they now are going to be dealing with the staff on a decision-

making level. It's important that this aspect of volunteer-staff relationships be discussed and understood.

5) People get to see that there's a team at work. The leaders may have been recruited individually by the President or some other person and can feel a little unsure of themselves. They need reassurance that they aren't out there alone trying to do the work of the organization. The orientation process allows leaders to see that support and assistance are available in many places and from many people.

It's important that this orientation process be as comprehensive as possible, but it also has to be an enjoyable experience. If volunteers are overwhelmed with rules, guidelines, organizational charts, job descriptions, and goals they are going to be discouraged before they even get started. Organizations need to avoid having "talking head" orientations, where one leader after another gets up and talks to the group about what his or her committee does, or how each line item in the budget is developed, etc., etc. The whole point of the orientation is to get volunteers off to a good, positive start in their leadership roles.

Taking a Resource Check

Since failing to adequately use all of their volunteers effectively is one of the reasons that organizations fail to meet their goals, the leadership orientation should also be used as a place to take a "resource check". This means taking time to learn more about the new (and carry-over) leaders and to find out what skills and talents they bring with them to the job. This *can* be accomplished by asking the volunteers what they think they can offer or what they believe to bè their greatest assets, but it's hard to get people to open up and talk about themselves in that manner.

Part of the reason organizations don't get more out of their volunteer leaders is that *they don't ask the right questions*. When the question is stated as "Who wants to work on the newsletter?" the response is pretty predictable. No one wants to volunteer for the responsibility of putting out a newsletter. If the question had been "Who likes to work on the computer, and has some experience with graphics?" the response might be completely different.

People are usually open about the things they like to do and the things at which they feel they are competent. By asking for information, rather than volunteers, leaders can start to match the people with specific skills or interests to jobs in which there is a high (or, at least higher) probability of success because the volunteers start with some level of confidence.

In the case of the people who like to work with computer graphics, there might be an opportunity to get them started by asking them to take the proposed articles for the next issue of the newsletter and try to put them into a good looking, easy to read format. That's all you want the person to do the first time. Give them a chance to be successful at some level (you'll probably get a very well-designed and attractive newsletter) before asking them to take on the bigger job of publishing an entire newsletter from start to finish.

When organizations fail to ask the right questions regarding a person's desire or ability to take on a leadership role, it's really just another example of management by assumption. The organization assumes that because the leaders are all from one field (i.e. engineers) or one type of background (i.e. farmers from rural areas) there are certain things that can be assumed about them. Engineers are not generally thought of as "salespeople" or "marketers". Farmers are not usually considered to be experienced speakers or presenters. These stereotypes cause organizations to lose out on some tremendous leadership talent. Remember, people bring something with them to the organization besides just their job skills. It's the responsibility of the organization and its leaders to find out what these resources are before attempting to solve the organizations' problems.

For example, take the situation of an engineering society or social service organization that has a variety of leadership needs. These include such areas as membership, program, fundraising, and training. In looking over the list of possible candidates for these jobs, it could be assumed that their backgrounds won't help much in some of these areas. It would be just as easy to pick "a good person" and hope that he or she can learn how to handle the leadership role through on-the-job experience. Here's where the right questions need to be asked. These questions might include:

Have you ever held an elected leadership position in a volunteer organization?
Have you ever been a leader in a Scouting organization?
Have you ever spoken before a large group?
Have you ever had an article or book published?
Have you taught any classes at any level?

All of these questions are important, yet none is as daunting as "Who wants to take on a leadership job?" Take the question about Scouting. Most people would be happy to admit if they had served as a Scoutmaster, Den Leader, Troop leader, etc. By knowing that a person has been in this leadership role in Scouting, you know that the person has been involved in:

- membership recruitment
- fundraising
- public presentations
- dealing with young people

- meeting planning
- communications
- training, etc.

Look at all the skills needed to be an effective Scout leader. Aren't these the same skills that were noted earlier as being desirable in a leader? Before trying to decide who to ask to take a job, start with a resource check and try to figure out who the best candidates are. Start them off with a good chance for success.

Who's In Charge Here?

The most basic reason for having the leadership orientation is to assure that misconceptions are cleared up and situations like the ABC debacle don't occur. To get the most out of the orientation, here are some do's and don'ts:

DO
- give everyone a chance to meet everyone else
- structure the program so that everyone is required to participate
- schedule the orientation for a time and place conducive to maximum attendance
- give the staff and newer leaders a chance to get to know each other
- allow some non-structured time for informal discussion and relaxation

DON'T
- rely on written materials to get the information out
- have a series of "talking heads" restate what is in the written guidelines
- put so much information into the orientation that attendees can't absorb it

- have the entire orientation done by one person (volunteer or staff)
- forget to thank everyone for participating
- assume that just because information has been presented it is also absorbed

One exercise, entitled "Who's In Charge Here?", has proved very helpful to many organizations. It combines many of the elements mentioned above: it's interactive, it covers most of the major areas of leadership responsibility, it adds a visual aspect to the presentation, and it allows participants to be part of the learning experience. This exercise basically involves having attendees fill in a leadership "grid". They are given a sheet like the following:

Who is responsible for the following in our organization?

Activity/Responsibility	Pres.	Ex. Dir.	Ex Cmte.	Board	Comm(s)	Other
SETTING POLICY						
DEVELOPING BUDGET						
RECRUITING COMMITTEE CHAIRS						
APPROVING BUDGET						
MEMBERSHIP RECRUITMENT						
SPEAKING FOR THE ORGANIZATION						
RUNNING MEETINGS						
FUNDRAISING						
MEMBERSHIP RETENTION						
DETERMINING EDUCATIONAL PROGRAMS						
LONG RANGE PLANNING						
HIRING THE E.D.						
FIRING THE E.D.						

In the previous example, Pres. refers to the top elected volunteer leader; Ex Dir refers to the top paid staff person (if there is one); Ex Cmte refers to the Executive Committee (if the organization uses one); Board refers to the organization's governing Board; Comm(s) refers to operating committees; and Other refers to any leadership group or individual not covered by the other categories. Participants are asked to go down the list of activities/responsibilities and then go across and indicate who they believe is responsible for that activity. They can check one or more for each activity, depending upon whether they believe that a single individual or group is responsible or if they feel it is a shared responsibility.

After participants have had a chance to complete the form on their own, they are asked to compare their answers with other participants. It is always interesting to see that no two forms are identical. This is the personification of management by assumption.

There are some important reasons why this exercise is so effective:

1) It is a lot more interesting to discuss subjects like structure and responsibilities in this manner than by listening to someone talk about them.
2) It gets everyone involved in the orientation.
3) It really doesn't matter what final list is developed. After discussing each item, the important factor is that everyone in the orientation agrees that this is the way that activity should be handled during this coming year.
4) People have to agree, and make commitments, in front of other volunteer leaders. This adds to the probability of each person making a real attempt to meet his or her responsibilities.

5) Although it seems as though this exercise is designed for new leaders, it actually helps to clear up misconceptions held by all leaders. It's amazing how often a person who has been in a leadership role for several years can be operating under an assumption that is incorrect regarding organizational policy or structure. This goes on until something doesn't get done, or is done incorrectly. At that point everyone starts pointing fingers and asking why. It's better to clear these things up at the beginning of the year (at the orientation). The ABC situation discussed earlier is a good example. It's doubtful that the organization authorized any or all of its Board members to speak to the press about internal matters, but that's just what happened. Board members assumed that they were empowered to speak on behalf of the organization. This situation could have been avoided if the topic of who speaks for the organization had been discussed and clarified at the beginning of the year.

6) Things change from year to year, depending upon who holds the various leadership roles. Last year's President may have assumed that fundraising was a staff responsibility. Next year's President may feel that fundraising is a responsibility of all volunteer leaders, especially Board members. Why have the new President come into a Board meeting and begin to chastise Board members for their lack of success in raising money only to have the Board members indicate that they didn't know they were supposed to be raising money? It would have made a lot more sense for the President to go through the major responsibilities of Board members at the orientation and emphasize that he or she expected the Board to get involved in fundraising during the year.

7) When this responsibility grid is filled in completely, it becomes a "picture" of the organization's leadership structure. It shows all of the leaders that there is a team of volunteers with individual and shared responsibilities, and

that these team members share a commitment to accomplishing something for the organization.

There are other aspects of leadership that need to be covered at the orientation, such as explanations of the organization's legal structure, the financial status and policies of the group, working with staff members (if applicable), and timetables for implementing programs. These should be covered through some form of discussion or presentation, and supported by some written documents.

There are two important points to remember about the follow up to any leadership orientation. First, before the orientation session is closed, be sure to ask if there are any questions or clarifications needed. That way the minutes of the meeting will accurately reflect the commitments made during the session. Second, if there are any key leaders who were not able to attend the session, be sure to assign someone to do a shortened version of the orientation with those people. It only takes a small group - or even one individual - with a misconception about roles and responsibilities to throw an organization's leadership back into the chaotic state of "management by assumption".

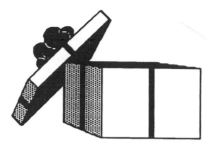

Chapter 7 - Leadership Training: The Giving of the Gift

This was one of the things that Karen had been looking forward to ever since her foundation had elected her as Board President. It was the group's first fundraising event of the year and she had every confidence that this was going to be a great event. The main reason for her confidence was Carol, the event's volunteer Chair. Not only was Carol a wonderful person and a generous giver to the foundation, she was Vice President of the local bank and well known in the community. On top of that, Karen had been sure to take all of the steps necessary to prepare Carol to run the event. She had recruited Carol carefully, making certain that Carol understood the importance of the event and the time it would take to put it on. Karen also assured Carol that there would be plenty of support from the staff and the other volunteers, but that she (Carol) had to be willing to take on the final responsibility of getting the job done. Carol had accepted the position willingly, and had mentioned that she felt good about the chance to help the organization in ways other than through writing a check. Carol also liked the fact that after the event was over she was through with her assignment (other than some follow up items).

Another reason for Karen's confidence in Carol was the fact that Carol had been an active participant in the Leadership

Orientation earlier in the year. Carol told Karen that she was impressed by how many other busy civic and professional leaders were at the orientation, spending their valuable time to help the foundation succeed. She also said she was pleased to see that Karen was a good delegator and was going to let the various committee and event chairs actually be in charge of their various functions and committees. Yes, Carol had told Karen, she left the orientation convinced that her work would be making an important contribution to the foundation and the people who benefited from the foundation's work.

As Karen walked into the hotel where the fundraiser was being held, she had a real sense of excitement. This was going to be a wonderful evening. Going though the lobby, she glanced at the Bulletin Board that listed the functions being held in the hotel that night. Sure enough, there was the foundation's fundraiser right at the top. Unfortunately, it said that the event would run from 6:30pm to 11:30pm. The invitations (and the budget!) called for the event to run from 7:30pm-10:30pm. Oh well, just a little mix up. No real problem.

The next thing Karen noticed was a long line outside of the ball room. She waited in the line, and after about 10 minutes she got to the front. There at the registration desk was Carol's daughter. She was by herself, trying to check everyone's invitation and then putting the attendees' names on the stick-on name tags. Inside the ballroom, Karen noticed another long line at the one bar that was set up in the back of the ballroom. In addition, it was terribly hot in the room, and there was no place for people to put their coats except on the backs of their chairs.

Just as Karen was starting to get a little concerned, she heard a screeching noise as Carol approached the microphone on the stage. Finally, someone got the volume turned down and

Carol gave her welcoming speech. Having seen Carol speak to groups before, Karen wasn't surprised when Carol gave a very nice welcome and thanks to the participants. O.K., Karen thought, everything is under control now. Until she decided to check on the food.

After waiting in another long line at the buffet table, Karen got up to the serving area to find that most of the more expensive foods - the shrimp, crab dip, shish-ka-bob, etc., - were already gone. The only things left were salad and a few cheeses. This was pretty upsetting to Karen, since it was only 45 minutes into the function. A number of people, including some of their biggest contributors, hadn't even arrived yet.

About 20 minutes later, Carol approached the microphone and started reading a list of people she wanted to thank for helping with the event. She also read a list of the "President's Club" contributors, people and organizations who had given at least $500 to the foundation. The lists were very extensive, and Carol waited until the applause for each person named was finished before reading the next name. It took a long time - nearly 30 minutes - to go through the list, but Karen figured since it was the only chance Carol had to publicly thank these people it was probably all right.

After the final names were read, Carol thanked everyone and said she hoped they had had a great time and would come again next year. Karen realized that Carol had forgotten to tell everyone when and where next year's function would be, or even how they could contribute to the foundation again. Perhaps even worse was the fact that two of the President's Club contributors had been left off the list of those receiving thanks from the podium. Karen saw both of them leave right after the announcements, and they didn't look too happy.

Finally, as Karen was getting ready to leave she walked back toward the front entrance only to see a long line of upset foundation attendees waiting for their cars to be retrieved from the hotel's garage. Karen wondered how someone as capable as Carol could forget to check on so many important details. After all, Karen had given Carol everything she needed to run the function - information, help, commitment, history, and encouragement. What happened?

What Karen didn't realize was that Carol had never run a big meeting in a big hotel for a large number of people with food, drinks, sound systems, and registration needs. Yes, Karen had recruited Carol the right way, and had given her a good orientation. Then she let Carol go to work on her project, and, like a good manager and delegator, stayed out of the way until Carol had a problem or asked for help. But Karen skipped a step between orientation and delegation. She skipped the training step.

She forgot about The Gift.

Knowing what's expected of you, and having the skills to do it, are two entirely different things. Training volunteer leaders isn't easy, but it is essential to improving their performance - and their sense of accomplishment. Leadership training is also the essence of the Gift of Leadership. In the long run, what people take away from their leadership roles is a total experience. That experience can be a good one or a bad one, but helping people develop skills that they can use outside of their volunteer role is bound to make the experience even more enjoyable and successful.

There are several reasons leadership training can be difficult for some organizations:
1) Many organizations don't know what type of training to provide.

2) Some groups aren't sure where to go for help in providing training.
3) For some organizations, it is hard to convince volunteers that they NEED training.

This last issue is probably the hardest one to overcome. After all, the leaders have given time from all of the other important events in their lives to work without pay for a voluntary organization. Then when they are ready to put in that time, they are told that they have to go for training.

For what, they are likely to ask. Training on how to put on a program? Training on how to run a committee? Who needs training on those things? They do those things all the time in their personal and professional lives. Is running a meeting going to be any different in this organization than running a meeting at an office?

Actually, it is. Everything is a little (or a lot) different in a volunteer setting. Training in various leadership areas not only points out these differences and helps the volunteer leader to deal with them, it also enhances skills in doing these things in other settings.

Even in organizations where leadership training is part of the regular operations, there is still the problem of convincing individuals that they need skill development. A person who has been in a managerial position is unlikely to believe that a volunteer organization can teach him or her much about delegation and employee motivation. Overcoming this attitude is difficult. The best way to do this is to "institutionalize" leadership training in the organization. Try to identify the skills most needed by ALL leaders and make training in these skill areas something that all leaders must take on an ongoing basis. That avoids the singling out of individuals and assures that all leaders get valuable training.

What Type of Training to Offer

If you go back to the chapter on proper recruitment you can look at the list of the skills that people said were most desired in a membership chair. Some of those skills are specific to the membership function (i.e. sales, marketing, etc.). Many of them, however, fall into that category of skills that would be helpful to someone in almost any leadership position. These are the skills on which organizations can build an ongoing leadership training program. A sampling of these universal skills:

• Presentation and Speaking Skills

This is perhaps the most useful skill for volunteer leaders and the one that is the most transferable to other areas of people's lives. Training in these skills can help leaders be more comfortable in front of groups large or small. It can also translate into an ability to make presentations to clients or client groups, improved performance in teaching and training situations, and (as was seen in the case of Joe) confidence to address other civic and volunteer groups such as service clubs, religious gatherings, and youth organizations. This skill area can even help people be more comfortable in social settings, thereby enhancing their personal lives.

• Facilitation Skills

Virtually all leaders will be required at some point to bring together other volunteer leaders in group settings. This occurs through committees, task forces, boards, and other decision-making groups. This ability to bring people together and get things done in an efficient manner is one of the skills most valued by managers and employers at all levels. Training leaders in effective group facilitation skills not only helps the organization run more smoothly, it helps the leader in charge and all of the participants feel that their time is well-spent and their leadership experience is worthwhile.

• Negotiating skills

This might seem like a very hard-nosed, business-type skill, but in reality volunteer leaders are involved in negotiating all the time. Some of the more typical negotiating situations in which leaders will find themselves include: negotiating with hotels or meeting sites over things such as dates, prices, rooms, etc.; negotiating with public officials on issues such as the funding of programs, individual projects, and support for various causes; and negotiating with other organizations to form working coalitions that will advance causes and serve more people. The ability - the skill - to negotiate effectively in these situations can mean the difference between success and failure for a leader and his or her organization.

There is another level of negotiating that leaders engage in all the time, yet many never realize that they are in a negotiating situation. This occurs when leaders engage in *negotiating needs*. Virtually every time volunteers work together for any organization, there is a needs negotiation going on.

As was discussed earlier, people serve for different reasons and sometimes those reasons, and the personalities behind them, come into conflict. The person who serves because volunteer leadership provides an opportunity for social interaction looks at his or her leadership role quite differently from the person who volunteered to accomplish a specific task and add to a resume. These two individuals might believe equally in the purpose or cause of the organization yet their needs come into conflict over and over. The effective leader will have (or will be given) the skill to recognize or identify the cause of the conflict and negotiate a situation that minimizes the appearance of having winners and losers.

• Delegation Skills

Why should a person's impact in an organization be limited to what he or she can do? Shouldn't a person's ability to make a difference depend more upon what he or she can *get done*? Volunteer organizations the world over are suffering from overworked and "burned out" leaders, and the reason isn't solely because there are no people to take their places.

Part of the shortage of volunteer leaders at the top of organizations is caused by the failure of the current leaders to acquire or use the skill of effective delegation. If the leaders brought this skill with them they could probably be successful. Many volunteers, however, don't have this basic skill. In that case, it becomes the responsibility of the organization to provide it.

• Membership and Fundraising Skills

There is a saying in business that "nothing happens until a sale is made." In many volunteer organizations, nothing happens until a member joins or a contribution is given. It seems natural that a volunteer who is active in an organization - a person who *believes* in the organization - would want to expand the organization and its impact by adding to its membership or financial base. After all, why would someone join or contribute to an organization and then be hesitant about asking someone else to do the same? When asked why they won't go out and raise money or recruit members, people generally give one of three reasons:
  • they don't have the time
  • they don't want to take advantage of a personal or

business relationship
- they're not salespeople and don't like "selling" or "begging"

One reason they probably *aren't* giving is the one reason that is probably the closest to the truth.

They're afraid.

They're not afraid of the time, they're not afraid of the effort, and they're not afraid to say the words.

They're afraid of the rejection.

No one wants to volunteer for rejection. People get enough rejection in their everyday lives without volunteering for more of it. (Just ask any parents of teenagers in the 1990's and they will tell you all about rejection. As the parent of two teenagers once said "If I want rejection I can go home. Easier yet, I can *call* it in!") The reason people fear rejection so much in the area of membership and fund raising isn't that they don't believe, and it isn't even that they don't know what to say to a prospective donor or member (after all, they have all of the organization's literature to guide them). The real problem for these people is the fact that the prospective donor or giver always has some questions or objections, and the volunteer doesn't know how to answer these.

Training volunteers in the skill of fundraising or membership is a great gift to give. This is truly a transferable skill and the effective leader will use it again and again.

• Planning Skills

If a volunteer leader comes from a business background, a teaching background, or some type of management background, he or she probably has some basic planning skills. However, many leaders don't come to their volunteer roles with an understanding of how important effective planning is and how much more efficiently an organization will run if it has a plan. Involving people in the planning process is a wonderful gift to give them because they can adapt some of the planning basics to their personal and professional lives. The leader who can successfully plan and implement a fundraising campaign for a voluntary, not-for-profit organization can probably help his or her company or institution in the areas of marketing, sales, and negotiating, in addition to planning.

Even organizations that don't want to get too "sophisticated" (due to lack of resources or time constraints) should set out annual goals and objectives as part of a basic plan of action. Informal planning is better than none at all but it doesn't take the place of a solid, manageable, more formal plan. The skills involved with effective planning can also be carried over to other leadership roles within the same organization or to another one.

These are only a few of the skills people need to be effective leaders. There are certainly others (remember the list of desired skills in a membership chair?). These skills - presentation and speaking skills, facilitation skills, negotiation skills, delegation skills, fundraising and membership skills, and planning skills are among the most important and will be helpful to most leaders. They are especially valuable to those who aspire to serve in the ranks of the organization's top leadership roles (President, Officer, Board member, etc.). As people move through the chairs of leadership these skills become cumulative and by the time they reach the top they have an excellent combination of on-the-job experience and skill development.

Chapter 8 - Getting People Involved

Steve had the best of feelings for Camp Devotion. The camp was important to Steve because it was a camp for children who suffered from a rare childhood disease, and that group included Steve's younger brother, Mike. Mike was among those who had enjoyed the great experience that Camp Devotion provided for these kids. Steve was grateful for the joy it had brought to Mike and he couldn't forget the look on Mike's face at the end of the camp program when Mike was given his award as The Friendliest Camper. Yes, Steve was certainly a "believer" in Camp Devotion, and the foundation that supported it.

Knowing of Steve's positive experience with the camp, Beth, the camp's director, felt certain that she could get Steve to accept a position on the camp's volunteer Board of Directors. When she approached Steve about serving, she was shocked to hear Steve say he was "just too busy" to serve as a volunteer leader. He'd be happy to make a contribution to the camp's fundraising efforts through the foundation, but he couldn't commit to serving in a leadership role. Maybe sometime "down the road" he had said.

How could someone who knew first-hand about the good work of the camp not want to serve in a volunteer leadership role? How busy could Steve really be, Beth wondered, that he wouldn't put in a few hours a month for an organization that had helped his family?

As was noted earlier, it's not a question of how much time people have to give - they all have the same 24 hours - it's a question of what they think they will accomplish in that time. Of course people today - people like Steve - are busy, but so is everyone else. Perhaps more than any previous generation, today's young adults have before them dozens of ways to fill up every waking hour. This creates a generation that not only cherishes "free time" but also one that sees any intrusion into that time as a threat to their own sense of self-control.

This attitude of being too busy can cause some consternation among leaders that have been active for a long time in an organization. They wonder how they could have enough time to commit to volunteer leadership but the next generation says that they're too busy to do the same. This attitude goes against the tradition of giving that most volunteer organizations have as their foundation. Leaders feel, "If volunteer service was good enough for me, why isn't it good enough for others?" While this feeling is certainly understandable, trying to get people to emulate the generation(s) before them has had little impact since the time of the ancient Greeks.

There's another reason why some people are reluctant to give up their time to a volunteer organization. Many of them truly want to volunteer and honestly feel that they would like to help give voice to their needs or beliefs. The problem is they *know* how busy they are, and if they say they will take on a leadership role there is every chance that they will not be able to live up to their commitment. They don't want to let anyone down, and they don't want the embarrassment of being "disciplined" for not living up to their promise to help. It's easier to say "no" than to put themselves in the path of failure or conflict.

Given all of this, there is still an opportunity to get people started in leadership and heading toward an understanding of The Gift.

Instead of assuming that members of the current (and future) generation(s) won't dedicate time to volunteer leadership, consider that perhaps they won't give *as much* time as the previous generation. This means that organizations need to tailor their approach to these people by keeping their concerns in the forefront. To tomorrow's generation of leaders, the term "serving on a committee" conjures up just one image - The Black Hole. They believe that saying "yes" to the offer of serving in a leadership role (such as a Committee Member) means that they'll spend night after night tied up with (unproductive) meetings, reading official organizational correspondence, and making telephone calls. They construe this to mean that they will never get to see their families or their home computers ever again.

Organizations will have to learn to change their traditional viewpoint of what "involvement" means. It will no longer be appropriate to think in terms of large investments of time when seeking leaders. Instead, leadership positions will have to be redefined and repackaged to meet the needs of the volunteer, not the need of the organization.

One concept that has become more popular in the volunteer community and has been borrowed from the private sector workplace is the concept of *job sharing.* If it is difficult to get one individual to accept a leadership role then it might be necessary - though certainly not traditional - to split the job between two people. They can either divide the responsibilities of the job or just split the time commitment. This situation calls for a great deal of understanding by the leadership group, and a lot of coordination among the individuals and the organization.

The alternative to this non-traditional approach to leadership is to hope that eventually someone will step forward and accept the bigger jobs, or that the current leaders will agree to pick up the extra work themselves. Neither of these options is going to solve the organization's long-term problem of having too few volunteers to take on all the bigger leadership jobs.

There is another way to deal with the issue of too little time, and it is somewhat contrary to traditional leadership thinking. This is a simple technique known as **"thinking small"**

Very few organizations set out to find the "small thinkers" in their midst. The opposite has always been true - organizations try to attract the "big thinkers" to leadership. They want leaders who see the big picture, plan for big improvements in the organization, and have the desire and ability to make a big commitment. Everyone wants these kinds of leaders but the reality is that there aren't enough of these big thinkers to go around.

Thinking small doesn't mean that there is no vision of a greater organization, doing greater good for more people. Thinking small is merely a realization that fewer and fewer people are available to take on big jobs. The effective volunteer organization in the modern setting needs to attract MORE people to leadership and the only way to do that is to break down the larger jobs into smaller ones. To think small actually takes more work, in many ways, than thinking big does. To have an effective organization with "small thinkers" there has to be more planning, more delegating, and more organizing. The goal of small thinking is to do three things: appeal to the need of newer leaders to serve but not to commit huge blocks of time; give these leaders a small taste of leadership success and introduce them to The Gift; and motivate them, through accomplishment and recognition, to take the next step in their commitment to volunteer leadership.

Here is an example of how thinking small could work in a typical organization. Assume that there is a membership or fundraising function within the organization. When the call goes out for volunteers - "Who would like to help us with our fundraising and membership work this year?" - the response is likely to be ear shattering silence. Instead of trying to get one or two people for the big jobs, maybe there is a chance here to get a number of people to take on a number of small jobs. Recruiting and fund raising can be daunting tasks, so break down the membership or fundraising *functions* and identify ways people can contribute (accomplish something) within those functions. In this case those tasks might include:

- helping to create a prospect list
- assisting in qualifying prospects (gaining additional information)
- hosting a meeting/function to meet prospects
- maintaining the organization's data base of prospective members/givers
- developing promotional literature
- writing solicitation letters
- telephoning current supporters for retention purposes
- calling new members or contributors to welcome them or say thank you
- working on a short-term campaign
- keeping records on members and givers
- coordinating public relations support for the campaign

This is a sample of one job broken down into smaller ones. It shows the chances that exist to get ten people involved in membership and fund raising, instead of just one or two. Would it be easier and faster to get one person to agree to take on all of these tasks? Of course it would, but where are these big job volunteers going to come from? The new reality of leadership in voluntary organizations is that the leadership role must be clearly defined, have a reasonable, achievable, and worthwhile outcome, and must fit into the volunteer's concept of a reasonable time commitment.

Leading the Non Leader

One group of volunteers that hasn't been discussed in any depth to this point is the group of volunteers who truly do NOT aspire to a "leadership" position. These people certainly want to contribute but they see themselves as volunteers, not necessarily as "leaders".

Is there a difference?

Certainly there is. "Leadership" has a connotation of some level of involvement in the organization's hierarchy, from a committee member to an officer. A person can be a volunteer without necessarily being involved in any way in the operation of the organization. Indeed, many people believe in the organization's work and simply want to make a contribution of some type. Rather than being concerned about the Gift of Leadership, these people tend to show up and say "What do you want me to do?" This basic approach to volunteering doesn't mean that they won't get involved in a leadership role sometime in the future, it just means they aren't at that point right now.

How can these people be motivated? If there is no interest in true leadership, how can they get The Gift?

Those who want to help but not get "involved" actually aren't that much different in their motivations than any other volunteers. They still want to do something worthwhile with their time. They still want to accomplish something. They still want recognition for their work. They may not see this volunteer involvement as a way to gain experience or expertise, and they may not be interested in any type of formal "training" but they *do* want to have a positive, successful experience. Motivation comes with success so even the smallest volunteer job needs to be accompanied by some sense of accomplishment. Organizations need to give these volunteers a feeling that whatever role they play is worthwhile in terms of helping the organization serve its constituents and give "voice" to those it represents.

Chapter 9- Volunteer Recognition: Delivering the Paycheck

Arlene loved doing her church work. The work gave her an opportunity to give something back to the institution that had provided her with so much support and comfort over the years. It also allowed her to socialize with some very nice people while doing something worthwhile for the church and the community.

Almost as importantly to Arlene, now that she had been asked to be on the church Board she was able to be an equal partner in decision-making with some of the community's business and social leaders. At work, Arlene considered herself just another member of the administrative staff. Oh, she liked where she worked well enough, and she had been there for a long time, but the work really wasn't very challenging. She liked to be part of making things happen from beginning to end, to see the "fruits of her labor".

That's why serving in the church leadership was so rewarding. In addition to feeling good about the work the church was doing, she now had a part to play in planning and carrying out church activities. As a Board member she would be able to actually get a taste of "leadership".

One of the events Arlene enjoyed was the church's Annual Dinner. It took place in late spring and was a celebration of all of the work done by the church throughout the previous year. Arlene liked the dinner because everyone was in a good mood and there was always a great turnout. She had worked on the dinner for many years, and had done just about every job connected with putting the program together. At first she helped serve the food, later she got involved with selling tickets, and the last few years she had been in charge of the entertainment. At the end of each dinner, Arlene and the other people who had worked on the dinner were "surprised" with a certificate of appreciation and a small bouquet of flowers (for the women) or some other gift for the men. Now that she was a Board member, Arlene felt a little awkward about getting those things at the dinner. She went to the Annual Dinner chairperson, Gene, to tell him not to worry about getting her anything.

"Gene," she said, "I do appreciate the little tokens that the committee gives each person at the dinner, but I'm a Board member now so I don't want the church to spend any money on a gift for me this year. I have a whole shelf full of the appreciation certificates, too. Just make sure the other people who work on the dinner get something nice. Don't worry about me."

Gene said that Arlene was being too modest and that her help <u>was</u> appreciated. The certificate and flowers were just the church's way of saying thanks, he explained.

"I realize that," Arlene replied, "but honestly, it's not necessary."

The night of the Annual Dinner came, and the function was a huge success. Everyone at the program had a wonderful time and at the end of the evening the Board Chair stood up to close the program.

"Before we adjourn," he said, "I want to be sure that we recognize all of the people who worked so hard to make this program go so smoothly. We have some certificates and gifts for those people who worked on the Dinner Committee this year."

After all the names were read off, the Chair asked all the attendees to give them a big round of applause. Finally, the Chair said "In addition to these fine people, I know that there are others who had a part in making this evening a success. Would all of you who helped work on the dinner in any way please stand up?"

Several people in the audience stood, but Arlene didn't. She didn't feel like getting some sort of "group" recognition. She had other thoughts going through her mind at that time. One of those thoughts was "After all I've done for this church, the best they can do is have me stand up with a group for three seconds."

It may seem as though Arlene didn't have much right to be upset. She did tell Gene not to bother getting her anything special in the way of recognition. Somehow, though, Arlene felt slighted after the event. In some ways, Arlene probably felt as though she had been given a "cut" in her "pay".

Recognition is the volunteer's paycheck, and it needs to be given in a timely and appropriate manner. When do you stop giving recognition? Never! Even in the case of people who, like Arlene, say that they don't want the recognition, there is a danger in asking them to work for absolutely nothing. When people stop getting "paid", eventually they will stop showing up for work.

Timely Rewards

Recognition for volunteer work shouldn't wait until the end of the year at some awards function. Even if an organization has some formalized recognition program, thanks should be given to volunteers as soon as it is appropriate to do so. In many cases, something as simple as a handwritten note or a phone call is all that is needed. Indeed, think what kind of impact it has when a person takes the time to phone someone for no other reason than to say "Thank you for volunteering." That phone call means so much more if it is made in a short time frame after the volunteer activity.

Immediate recognition doesn't mean that the organization can't thank workers again at a later time and in another manner. A note or phone call at the time of the service, and a mention of the person's name again at an awards function or in the organization's publication, is a great combination. It shows the person who volunteered that the organization not only appreciates the help but that the organization doesn't forget its supporters.

Let's Get Personal

It's also important that recognition be very specific and personalized. "Thanks for helping out" is fine, but if the intent is to motivate people to continue participating in a volunteer role then the recognition should be meaningful. When recognizing volunteers for their help, organizations should try to be specific about what contribution the person made and how that contribution helped the organization *accomplish* something.

If volunteers feel they have had a role in assisting in the organization's success they are much more likely to be involved again in the future - maybe at a higher or more time intensive level. Instead of saying "Thanks for helping out," the message should be "Thanks for picking up the decorations for the Awards Dinner. Those decorations made the meeting hall look like a fancy ballroom, and put everyone in a great mood. You really helped make the evening a success. I hope we can call on you to help us in the future."

The phone call is only one way of recognizing volunteer contributions. Some others include:

Organizational Publications

Most volunteer organizations have some sort of publication that is sent to their members, supporters, or contributors. These publications can be used as a vehicle for giving recognition to volunteers for their work within the organization. One group has a monthly column entitled "Tip of the Hat". It's the organization's "thank you" column. In each issue they list volunteers who have worked for the organization, they identify specifically what they are being thanked for, and, where appropriate, they identify either the volunteer's employer or the area of the community in which they live.

People love to see their names in print, so just the fact that they are listed in this column is a source of recognition. Not only does the volunteer get recognition from the organization, he or she probably has friends and/or coworkers who will see the publication, too. There is a good chance that some of these people will take the time to add their congratulations to the volunteer.

Another way to use the organization's publications for recognition is to take group photos of volunteers who deserve recognition and put these photos in the publications. While not as powerful as individual recognition, a photo does let people see the volunteer and allows more volunteers to be recognized. Perhaps the best way to use a group photo for recognition would be to write a short personal note to the volunteers to thank them for their work. Then add a P.S. to inform them that their picture is going to be in the next issue of the organization's publication.

Employer Recognition

Volunteers can also be recognized through their place of employment. The volunteer organization can find out who the volunteer's employer/supervisor is and drop a note to that person telling of the fine work that their employee is doing within the organization, community, etc. The employer will inevitably mention getting the note to the employee, who will think highly of the organization. It is a wonderful reinforcement of the value of volunteering.

Some larger companies have their own in-house publications, usually some type of employee newsletter. If a volunteer organization knows that one or more of its volunteers works for a company with such a publication, they can send a note to the editor of that publication explaining what type of contribution the employee has made. It has to make a person feel great if one or more of his or her coworkers says that they saw a note in the employee newsletter about their involvement in a volunteer organization. There is even the possibility that someone else in the company will become interested in the organization and ask about ways to participate.

Public Recognition

In some communities, volunteer organizations have a great opportunity to recognize their volunteers through local newspapers and other media. Most local papers actively look for information about local citizens who are in leadership roles in various organizations. Volunteer groups should try to identify the key staff people on these papers and get to know them. Visit the editor of the business or community section of the local paper and tell him or her about the work of the organization. Leave a "fact sheet" with contact names. Then, whenever a volunteer does something noteworthy within the organization - winning an award, being appointed to a leadership role, etc. - send a note to that contact at the local paper. If space is available it is just possible that the information and recognition will show up in the next edition of the paper.

In addition to news releases or articles about the work of volunteer leaders, the organization can try sending photos of individual leaders or groups of volunteers to the local papers. Depending upon the amount of space available and the relationship between the organization and the newspaper staff, there is a chance to get these photos published and to give volunteers some much-deserved recognition.

Part III
A Surprise Package of Gifts

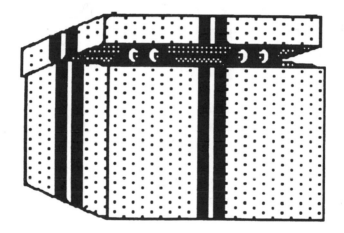

Chapter 10 - Facilitation Skills:
We've Got to Stop Meeting Like This!

Alice was about to hold the first committee meeting of her year as Committee Chair. She had worked on the committee for a couple of years and was glad to be the new Chair since she had some specific ideas on what the committee should be doing and how it should be run. Even though the committee members knew that they met on the third Thursday of each month (except July and August) she had sent out a reminder notice. In the notice she told people to be on time, since there was a lot to cover, and had attached a draft agenda.

ABC Organization
Committee Meeting Agenda
7:00pm - ?????

Opening Comments
Minutes From Previous Meeting
Financial Report
Old Business
    1. Site selection for spring program
    2. Report on status of fundraising project
New Business
    1. Calendar of events
    2. Menu selection for dinner meeting
    3. Scheduling activities for coming year
    4. Reports from Task Forces
Other Business (open discussion)
Report from National Headquarters
Final Comments
Adjournment

There were 8 people on the committee, and she was confident of a 100% turnout for this first meeting. She was all settled in the conference room at her office, where the meeting was to be held, waiting for the committee members. And waiting. And waiting.

About five minutes before the official starting time, only four of the eight members had arrived. Alice decided to wait a few more minutes. Fifteen minutes after the original starting time, everyone was there except Bill. Alice hated to start without Bill, since he probably knew more about the organization than anyone on her committee. Still, she thought, we can't wait all night, so she called the meeting to order.

"Thank you all for coming," she said. "We've got a lot to discuss, so we'll get right to the minutes of the last meeting. Julie, would you please read them for us?"

Before Julie could even open her mouth, Alan jumped in.

"You know," he began, "that just reminded me of the time we had that meeting where the roof leaked and got the papers all wet. It was really a riot. Some of you weren't around then, but let me tell you..."

Alice realized that Alan was off to the races with one of his war stories, so she interrupted him. "That was a funny meeting, Alan, but we've got an awful lot to cover. If we expect to get out of here at a reasonable time we have to keep on track. Julie, please go on."

Just then Bill came in. "Sorry I'm late," he said. "Traffic was terrible. What did I miss?"

Alice quickly reviewed the discussion up to that point. "We're glad to see you, Bill. Well, we haven't done very much so far.

I started off by thanking everyone for coming, and then Julie started to read the minutes but Alan wanted to tell some of the newcomers about the time we had a leaky roof. I told Alan that we had an awful lot to cover so we went ahead with Julie's reading of the minutes and that's when you came in."

They went through the agenda items one by one. The meeting never seemed to flow, however. If it wasn't someone getting off track it was someone else dominating the discussion. At least Alan wasn't a problem. In fact, he didn't have much to say. For that matter, neither did the two new committee members, Grace and Ed. Maybe the biggest disappointment for Alice was what happened when it came time to discuss the topics for the next program. Each person was given plenty of time to tell how he or she felt about the program content, and why he or she felt that way. Again, only about half the committee had anything to say, and they had numerous opposing viewpoints. The biggest dispute was over the funding of the programs. It seemed as though half the committee wanted to fund it through an assessment and the other half wanted to take it out of the organization's reserves. When it looked as if there was no way to make a decision, someone on the committee turned to Alice and said "You're the committee chair. What do you think we ought to do?"

Alice wanted to be fair, but she also had a pretty good idea about how she thought the program should be funded. She tried to choose her words carefully.

"I'm just the committee chair," she stated. "I don't even get a vote unless it's a tie. I think an assessment would be stupid at this point. Now, why don't we vote on it."

Not surprisingly, the committee voted to fund the program out of the reserves.

Finally, they got through most of the agenda items. Alice said that it was getting so late they would have to get together again in a couple of weeks to finish up on some important items. She would let them know when the next meeting would be held.

A couple of weeks later she sent out another cover note and agenda (one that was almost identical to the previous one) about the next meeting and asked everyone to come prepared to work. The meeting would be at the same time and at the same place.

This time, only three people showed up. Not enough to conduct business - no quorum - so Alice told the others to go home. It was obvious to Alice that she had some big problems with her committee. What did she do wrong, she wondered?

Alice may not think she had made a lot of mistakes, but she had. She felt that her experience in holding staff meetings at her office had given her plenty of experience in small group facilitation and decision-making, which it probably had. There is a difference between running a meeting of your staff and running a meeting of your leadership peers. The main difference is that the people at the leadership meeting *don't have to be there!* Understanding the nature of this difference and working to overcome it takes some very specialized leadership skills.

Leadership on Trial

As part of a study conducted by Hofstra University on the impact of meetings in the workplace, 803 managers in large U.S. corporations were asked to describe their feelings about staff meetings. A vast majority found these meetings to be time consuming and unproductive. In fact, when the researchers analyzed the amount of time spent in corporate staff meetings it was determined that in the United States alone over *$37 billion* in wages is wasted annually through unproductive staff meetings! When obtaining responses to determine why managers felt the meetings were unproductive, 1/3 said that they felt they had no impact on the ultimate decision that was made, and another 1/3 said they felt pressure to back opinions with which they privately disagreed.

Volunteer organizations need to take note of this information because when leadership meetings are not effective they waste people's time, and they waste people's money. As was discussed in the section on getting people to volunteer, it's this wasting of time that drives people away from volunteer leadership. A great amount of time is spent getting people to volunteer their valuable time, and when they finally show up to give their time they very often wind up in a meeting that wastes it.

There was one other aspect of the Hofstra study that is critical to volunteer organizations. In the survey of managers attending meetings, it was found that three out of four attendees judged others by how they behaved at these meetings, meaning that they judged their peers on their behavior at decision-making meetings. Most dramatic was the fact that a full *87% judged a person's leadership capabilities by how he or she ran a meeting*.

Transferring this information to a voluntary organizational setting sends a very clear message to those organizations. When you put a volunteer in charge of a committee (Board, task force, etc.) you are putting that person's leadership skills on trial in front of his or her peers! If the organization is going to do that, then it has a huge obligation to be sure that the volunteer leader is trained to be successful in that role. Perhaps more than anywhere else in the world of volunteer leadership, this is the place leaders want - and deserve - The Gift.

The Value of "Committees"

Before discussing effective methods for managing committees
and facilitating decisions, it's important to understand why
voluntary organizations use group decision-making
(committees) as a way to run their organizations. For purposes
of this discussion, the term committee refers to any small
decision-making group - boards, task forces, operating
committees, etc. There are actually several important reasons
why the committee structure is important to a volunteer
organization:

1) Committees allow for varied opinions and viewpoints.
   They should be representative of a cross section of the
   organization's membership or supporters and assure that
   there are ample opportunities for the diverse aspects of the
   group to be represented.
2) The committee structure helps share the workload. Even in
   organizations with large, full time professional staffs more
   work can be done if a system of effective committees is
   taking on part of the workload. Committees, in many
   organizations, are the structure through which the
   leadership is able to delegate some of the work.
3) Committee involvement gives people a sense of ownership.
   This is invaluable in helping create a group of dedicated
   and committed leaders. People who are involved in
   deciding what the organization is going to do are much
   more likely to be committed to making those things
   happen than people who are not involved.
4) Committees provide a training ground for future leaders.
   Many of the leaders of tomorrow are getting their
   leadership start at the committee level. If there is no
   committee structure, then people are forced to enter
   leadership situations at the highest (i.e. Board) level with
   no prior experience in any leadership role. This is a

difficult jump for some people to make, and the committee structure gives them a starting place that is more comfortable. At the same time, getting new leaders involved on committees gives current leaders a chance to evaluate the leadership potential of newer people. They can identify those with the skills and characteristics they desire in a leader. They can also identify the skills that are lacking in potential leaders and begin giving them the Gifts that will make them even better leaders by the time they reach higher levels within the organization.

5) Committees foster better use of the organization's human resources and help make better decisions by combining the expertise of the committee members. Rather than just hoping an individual has all the skills, characteristics, experience, and knowledge necessary to make good decisions in a particular area, the committee structure enhances the chances that those elements exist collectively in the committee.

When taken together, these reasons form a powerful argument for using committees effectively in volunteer organizations. Does this system have any drawbacks? Most certainly. Some of the more obvious drawbacks include:

1) TIME. It takes longer to get things done through a committee than it does when one or two people are in charge of a product or service.

2) The committee structure also invites conflict. When a committee of seven people meets there are dozens of ways to disagree. The more people on the committee, the more chances there are for people to disagree.

3) Sometimes committees will take risks that individuals might not take on their own. There is a sense of security that comes from group decisions because no one person will be held responsible for the group's actions.

Anticipating Problems

To take advantage of all of the *positive* reasons for having committees, leaders should anticipate the things that can go wrong at committee meetings and prepare to limit the impact of these problems or eliminate them altogether. As indicated by the attendees at leadership sessions around the world, the most common complaints about meetings are:

- meetings don't start on time
- one person dominates the discussion
- some people don't participate at all
- people come to the meeting unprepared
- someone becomes defensive or argumentative
- there is no agenda, or the meeting doesn't stick to it
- no decisions are made
- the discussion gets bogged down in personality conflicts and hidden agendas

There are other things that can go wrong, but these are the most common problems mentioned. When people give up their valuable time to come to a meeting where these things occur, they can come to only one conclusion - what a waste of time! Of course, wasting their time is the one thing that volunteer leaders absolutely do NOT want to do.

Whose job is it to reduce or eliminate these "meeting killers"?

It's the chairperson's job.

Whose job is it to make certain that the chair person is trained to handle these problems?

It's the organization's job.

Using the Meeting Agenda Effectively

One of the most effective tools for overcoming some of the meeting problems is the meeting agenda. Most people think that the agenda has only one purpose, and that is to determine the order in which items will be discussed. That is certainly an important use of the agenda, but it is only one of several uses it has. The agenda, in addition to determining the order of items, should also:

- help people prepare for the meeting
- encourage meeting attendance
- serve as a management tool for the committee chair once the meeting starts

If you look at the agenda sent out by Alice in the scenario described at the beginning of this chapter, you'll note that it probably looks similar to agendas used in many organizations. That agenda, however, covers only one of the purposes of a good agenda, the listing of the order in which things will happen. To take advantage of the other aspects of a good agenda, here are some suggestions.

1) Send the agenda, along with the meeting notice, far enough in advance of the meeting that people can use it as a reminder that they have made a commitment to attend.

2) Send as much support material with the agenda as you possibly can. This will help the attendees prepare to discuss items more thoroughly and will eliminate the need for attendees to read through everything for the first time at the meeting.

3) If you want to use a "timed" agenda, don't put exact times on the items (i.e. 7:15-7:30). This creates too much pressure to stay on schedule and eliminates some of the Chair's flexibility in running the meeting. Put the amount of

time allotted for each item (i.e. 10 minutes) and use those as a general guide for controlling discussion. Another suggestion would be to have these times only on the agenda of the Chair (and perhaps the staff liaison).

4) Consider using a consent agenda. This is a technique which allows a number of items which require no discussion to be passed at the same time. Some of the things to include in the consent agenda might be previous minutes and written reports submitted by committees or others not at the meeting.

5) To use the agenda to help promote attendance, add a section identified as "Purposes" at the top of the agenda. This section is a series of short statements that describe what action will be taken at the meeting. It reinforces that there are important matters on the agenda and that there needs to be a decision made on them at this meeting. That's the reason for the meeting - to make decisions, not to discuss things. (Note: If you're having trouble articulating the action needed at the meeting, you might want to reevaluate the necessity of having this meeting in the first place).

6) As often as possible, try not to add anything to the agenda from the time it is sent until the time of the meeting. It isn't fair to tell people the meeting will cover certain topics only for them to show up and find that there are matters being covered other than the ones for which they prepared.

Here's a sample of an agenda for a typical Board meeting.

Board of Directors Meeting
ABC Organization
November 7, 1999
Hometown, Ohio

Purposes: The purposes of this meeting include:
1) Acting on the recommendations from the Membership Committee
2) Adoption of the Annual Budget
3) Approval of the proposed educational programs
4) Selection of the representatives to the international meeting
5) Approval of proposed Bylaw Changes

AGENDA

1. Opening Comments . . . . Mike Salisbury, President
2. Review/approval of Previous Minutes* . . . . . . Bill Smith, Secretary
3. Review of Financial Reports . . . . Jane Flowers, Treasurer
4. Adoption of Annual Budget*
5. Membership Committee Recommendations* . . . . . Tom Smith, Chair
6. Approval of Educational Programs* . . . . Edith Jones, Chair
7. Approval of Proposed Bylaw Changes* . . . . Dean Allison, Chair
8. Update on Committee Activities
    Nominating
    Finance
    Promotion
    Annual Meeting
    Membership
    Sponsorship
    Program
    Publicity
    Advocacy
9. Selection of Representatives to International Meeting*
10. National Council Report . . . . Charlene Jacobs
11. Executive Director's Report . . . . Mike Lewis
12. Review of Annual Awards Dinner Activities . . . . John Callison
13. Adjournment

* Indicates items which require Board action or voting

Getting people to come to committee meetings is often a difficult task, but it's nothing compared to the biggest challenge of all - the challenge of having an effective meeting where things actually get done. Some of the problems with committees can be traced to administrative problems - agenda problems, location problems, distractions, etc. The main reasons meetings are a waste of time are directly related to the *behavior* of those in attendance. Dealing with these behaviors effectively takes patience and skill.

Why Do People Act Like That?

Once the meeting starts, the Chair will determine the success of the meeting and the sense of accomplishment felt by the attendees. To ensure the smooth operation of the committee, the Chair should consider the possible problems from his or her particular committee members and plan what action to take should those problems arise. Here are some possible scenarios and suggestions on how to handle them. Note that in addition to identifying what is happening, it's also important to try to understand *why* these behaviors occur.

The Problem: One person is dominating the meeting.

The Possible Reasons: This is a very common occurrence, and one that challenges the leadership abilities of the Chair. The initial response to this problem is usually to interrupt (politely) the person dominating the meeting at some point and say something like "Thanks for your input, but we really need to move on." This seems a simple enough solution because the Chair has now regained control of the meeting and can get back to the important items on the agenda. However, it is wise to think before acting in a situation such as this one. Why would someone volunteer to be on a committee, come to a meeting and do all the talking?

There could be several reasons for this behavior. The person could be looking for attention. The person could have a number of things he or she feels strongly about and wants to make certain his or her viewpoint is heard. Or, the person may not get as much attention at home - or at work - as he or she gets by being a volunteer leader in the organization!

Some people actually look forward to meetings and gatherings of their volunteer organizations because they get something out of those organizations that they don't get in other parts of their lives. For these people, even a simple statement such as "We need to move on" sounds a lot like "shut up". In this case, while the Chair has now regained control of the meeting, the other person has been disciplined in front of his or her peers and friends. That person is probably thinking "And after all I've done for this organization, they tell me to shut up." With just a few words the Chair has taken away the very reasons this person volunteered in the first place.

Possible solution: The Chair has to understand what's going on and act appropriately. If in controlling the meeting another member is made to feel slighted, the Chair has created a situation where there is a winner and a loser. In a volunteer organization, that's a dangerous and unproductive way to operate.

One solution to this problem is to use the meeting agenda as a management tool for the Chair. The Chair can interrupt the dominant member and say something such as "That's an interesting point. Why don't you hold on to that idea until we get down to the open discussion part of the meeting. That would be the appropriate time to bring that up. In fact, I'll make a note to call on you for further input on that when we get to it on the agenda. For now, let's return to the question at hand."

In this case, the Chair has actually conveyed several messages. First, the Chair has assured the member that his or her viewpoint will be heard, this just isn't the appropriate time for that particular topic. The Chair has even indicated when the member will speak on that topic. Second, the Chair has signaled to everyone that the meeting is under control. Third, the Chair has made it clear that the agenda was established as the order of business and that's what the meeting will adhere to. These are all positive signals to be sending.

The Problem: A member of the committee is not participating at all.

Possible Reasons: The person may be shy. The person may be new and uncertain about his or her role in the group. The person may be intimidated by another member of the committee.

Possible solutions: The first thing many think about this situation is, so what? This is (usually) an adult who has volunteered to serve in a leadership role. If he or she doesn't want to participate, so what? Let those who do want to participate have their say and move on with the meeting.

The reason that it's important to try to get everyone to participate at a meeting is not just because it's the polite and appropriate thing to do. The most important reason to get people to participate is that they may have something to offer to the discussion that can help the group make a better decision. The Chair <u>owes</u> it to the committee to make sure the committee is using all of it's available resources and information.

If the person is not participating because he or she is shy, the obvious way to draw that person out would be to ask him or her a direct question to encourage participation. Even a solution as seemingly simple as this needs some thought. If the Chair turns to the shy person and says "Jay, we haven't heard much from you yet, what do you think about that?" it may have the opposite effect of the one desired. Jay is now put on the spot and feels that everyone at the meeting is looking at him. Is putting a spotlight on a shy person really the way to make him or her feel comfortable? If the Chair tries to ask a non-threatening question, such as "Jay, why don't you tell us more about your family?", it may get Jay talking but it's out of context with the rest of the meeting.

One technique that may work in this situation is to go around the table and ask for *everyone's* input on a topic. The Chair can say "This is an important issue, and I'd like to hear everyone's opinion on this. We'll go around the table, and to keep things moving I'll limit each comment to 30 seconds." Of course, the Chair wouldn't want to start with Jay. By the time it is Jay's turn to express himself he knows he's not being singled out, he has time to collect his thoughts, and he feels as though his opinion is valued by the group.

If the person is not participating because he or she is new to the group and isn't certain about his or her role, then the Chair and the organization need to realize that the problem here may be the organization, not the member. New people should feel comfortable being full participants at their first meeting. It makes no sense for a person to have to attend several meetings before feeling confident enough to speak up. Look at all of the valuable input the committee loses while waiting for these new people to catch up.

An effective solution to this problem is to anticipate it and avoid it altogether. The Chair should invite people attending their first meeting to arrive 20-30 minutes before the starting time. The Chair (or a designated committee member) can sit down with the new people and go through the agenda with them, giving them background information and explaining the issues. There should also be a discussion about how the meetings are run so that the new people are comfortable with the Chair's style.

During this pre-meeting session, the Chair can get to know more about the new members and note where they might have something important to add to the discussion during the upcoming meeting. Finally, the Chair can actually ask the new person(s) if it would be all right to call on him or her at a certain point in the meeting to give input on a particular issue. This prepares the new person(s) and allows him or her to give some thought to what to say.

If the person is not participating because he or she is intimidated, there are a couple scenarios that may be taking place. The person could be intimidated because the other people at the meeting have a (perceived) higher position in the industry, profession, or community. If this is the case, the Chair can ease the intimidation by placing name cards at each person's place. That way people will tend to call each other by name, and that eases the formality of the interaction.

Another possibilty to consider is the possibility that people may not be participating because they are intimidated not so much by an individual as they are by the way the meeting is conducted. Indeed, it's possible that a person might be willing to participate but after watching the Chair discipline someone (i.e. the dominant person) earlier in the meeting he or she might now be afraid to speak up for fear of being disciplined in front of peers. This is a case where the inappropriate handling of one situation has caused problems in another situation.

The Chair is also faced with the problem of worrying so much about the non-participant that the meeting's focus is lost. A lot of time is spent trying to draw out those who don't participate and that can cause frustration among those on the committee who are participating and who want to move on.

After trying various techniques to get everyone involved, the Chair does have to move on and allow those who are willing to participate to do so. The Chair owes it to the group to make every attempt to use all the resources of the group but there is only so much that can be done.

The Problem: One of the committee members becomes defensive or argumentative.

The Possible Reasons: There can be several reasons why people participating in volunteer leadership roles would become argumentative at a meeting. One reason could be a feeling that their viewpoint is being attacked. They may also feel that their input isn't being given the credibility it deserves. It is also possible they are not happy with the direction in which the discussion is going.

Possible Solutions: This is a very difficult situation for the Chair. It's imperative to keep the meeting going in the right direction, but there is a danger in cutting off a member who is already being defensive. The Chair has to understand that the issue here isn't the topic under discussion, it's the immediate need(s) of the participants. The individual in this case is challenging the Chair's control of the situation and the Chair, again, needs to avoid the appearance of winners and losers.

To turn this situation around and keep things on a positive level, the Chair needs to use common sense and restraint. One technique that might help is to paraphrase what the individual is saying and repeat his or her thoughts. For instance, the Chair might say "Let me be sure that we understand what you're saying. Is it your contention that we shouldn't move forward until we have the final audit?" If the Chair repeats one or two of the exact words the person used, that's even better. This technique doesn't require that the Chair *agree* with the person, only that the person be assured that the Chair is *listening* to him or her.

Another option would be to ask the person to put his or her argument in writing and distribute it to the rest of the committee prior to the next meeting. That way the current meeting can move forward while the person feeling threatened will be sure that his or her opinion isn't being ignored or misinterpreted.

The Problem: Discussions are getting bogged down in a personality conflict.

The Possible Reasons: This one is hard to analyze. Two people may engage in inappropriate behavior because they just don't like each other. They may argue because of a previous incident or situation that has nothing to do with the meeting at hand but has carried over to this meeting. Whatever the cause, this is a fairly common situation and one that causes considerable stress on the meeting. Personality conflicts also cause considerable embarrassment to the entire group, not just the individuals involved in the conflict. Personality conflicts rarely manifest themselves in one meeting or encounter. They build up over time and that means the tension between the individuals, and the entire committee, continues to build, too. The Chair has to diffuse this situation not only to get the meeting going and to stop the participants from dominating meeting time, but also to assure that other members of the committee don't get fed up with the disruptive behavior and stop participating themselves.

Possible Solution: Assuming that the personality conflict is an ongoing problem, the first thing the Chair can do is make it physically awkward for the antagonists to keep their conflict going. The one thing that the Chair *doesn't* want is to have these people sitting across a table from each other. When they can read each other's body language and respond in kind it will just heighten the conflict. The Chair should assign or request that the people in question sit on the same side of the table next to each other. This will make it more difficult for the two individuals to argue because they will have to be physically close to each other.

Another technique the Chair can use is to find issues on which the two people do agree. When the Chair points out that in addressing the issues - which is the whole purpose of the committee - they agree on several things, it takes the meeting back into the area of decision-making and out of the area of personalities. Of course, the best place to handle personality conflicts is not at the committee meeting but away from the meeting or between meetings. Unfortunately, some people will take advantage of the structured discussion of a committee meeting to push their conflict with other individuals because they feel some security in the group. That's the time when the Chair is challenged to come up with an equitable and immediate solution.

The Problem: People come to the meeting unprepared.

The Possible Reasons: The most obvious reason a person would come to a meeting unprepared is the fact that he or she didn't read the material sent ahead of time. This assumes that the Chair or someone else has sent material to the attendees prior to the meeting.

There are some other possible reasons why a person might attend a meeting unprepared. One might be that the person is new to the committee and doesn't have the background he or she needs. Another factor that might create the appearance of people being unprepared is the situation where either there was no agenda sent prior to the meeting or there have been changes in the agenda since the pre-meeting agenda was sent.

Possible Solutions: A meeting agenda and background materials should be sent to the meeting attendees at least one-two weeks prior to each meeting. In addition to the agenda and background materials all attendees should have received a copy of the minutes from the previous meeting. The minutes and agenda should highlight issues that will require action at the upcoming meeting. If any of the attendees will be making special reports at the meeting, a reminder to that person should be sent ahead of time, along with a clear delineation of how much time that person has been allotted at the meeting.

For newer people the suggestion (again) is to ask them to arrive a few minutes before the other attendees and have the Chair bring them up to date on the issues that will be addressed by the committee at the upcoming meeting.

The agenda itself should make it clear to the attendees what the priorities of the meeting are and what issues will be discussed and/or decided. If the members need further information they should be given the name of someone to contact for assistance prior to the meeting. Once the agenda has been sent to the attendees, there should be no changes made. It is very disconcerting to receive one agenda in the mail and then show up at the meeting and find an amended or altered agenda on the table.

The Problem: No decisions are made.

The Possible Reasons: Of all the problems that occur at committee meetings, the inability to reach decisions may be the most harmful. After all, this is the main reason that people attend - to decide what is going to happen within the organization and to be a part of the organization's leadership. When no decisions are reached it's frustrating (and a waste of time!) for everyone. This doesn't mean that the Chair should see reaching a decision as so important that the other values of committees (ownership, input, expertise, etc.) should be forgotten. The goal of the committee is to reach decisions and the role of the Chair is to see that that is accomplished in an efficient and effective manner.

Frequently the reason decisions are not reached, or that they are reached under very short time constraints, is that the meeting hasn't been properly run. All of the previous problems - dominant members, non-participants, personality conflicts, etc. - have taken up so much of the committee's time that decision making is reduced to a matter of expediency. The Chair promised in the pre-meeting information that decisions were going to be made and the Chair now feels obligated to reach those decisions within the allotted time frame. This can lead to hasty decisions and people feeling that there was inadequate discussion before a vote was taken.

Another reason that decision-making can be difficult in volunteer organizations is that committee members sometimes defer to the Chair, or the staff person (if one is present), when a final decision needs to be made. The members often feel that the Chair (or staff) will have the ultimate responsibility for carrying out the committee's work, so that person should have the final say on what the committee will do or recommend.

Possible Solutions: This situation, where the meeting keeps going on and no decisions are made, really hits at the need for the committee Chair to develop some facilitation skills. All of the good work that has gone before - getting people to participate, using the agenda properly, controlling discussion, etc. - can be erased if the decision-making process isn't handled properly.

The first thing to consider is whether or not the Chair should make his or her feelings known on a topic before the group decides. Remember, it's not the Chair's job to do the work of the committee. The Chair's job is to get the work of the committee done. However, the Chair has been selected because he or she has the skills and characteristics that the organization wants in a chairperson, so the Chair absolutely IS entitled to input. In fact, the Chair has some obligation to express his or her views before the group moves on and decides the final disposition of a topic. The Chair does have to be careful about how that input is given. If the Chair indicates that he or she prefers a particular course of action, or is adamant that there is a "right" decision, there is a risk that those who don't agree with the Chair's viewpoint will feel that the decision of the committee was based on what the Chair wanted to do, not on what the committee wanted to do. These people can leave the meeting feeling that the process didn't work - that they were forced to accept a decision with which they didn't agree. In short, they don't feel any "ownership" of the decision. What's the Chair to do?

A technique that has worked for many volunteer leaders involves several steps. Step one is to summarize the discussion up to that point. By doing so the Chair shows everyone that he or she was listening to others' input before making a suggestion. Steps two and three are to give input and then get "out" of the discussion without controlling it. The Chair can say something like "I've been listening to all of the discussion on this matter, and those for it seem to feel this way while those against seem to feel the other way. Based on what I've heard, I'm not sure that we should be moving ahead with this project, but before we vote, let's go around the table and get everyone's final thoughts. We'll limit these comments to 30 seconds from each person."

What the Chair has done in this case is to give his or her opinion but not a directive or decision. By going back around the table, the Chair gives each committee member another chance to express his or her view before a final vote is taken. The members also know what the Chair thinks about the issue but don't feel required or obligated to vote the way the Chair thinks. By putting a time limit on each comment, the Chair also assures that the last comments before the vote won't be too time consuming.

The issue of the staff person's input into volunteer decision-making is always a touchy one. In a volunteer organization, should the staff be telling the members what to do? Isn't it the staff's job to carry out the wishes of the volunteer leadership? The answer to these questions isn't a simple yes or no.

On the question of whether or not the staff should be carrying out the wishes of the leadership, the answer is *of course*. The important thing is whether or not the wishes and decisions of the leadership are based on the best information. That brings us back to the first question about whether or not the staff should be telling the leadership what they should be doing.

The staff's role is not to tell the members what they should do. The staff's job is to be sure that the volunteers are making their decisions with all of the information that the resources of the organization can provide. The staff's job in decision making can be identified as having three components:

1) Information. This is the number one reason the staff of any volunteer organization is paid.
2) Options. The staff should be sure that the volunteer leaders are aware of what options are available to them in various situations. This doesn't mean that the leaders have to limit themselves to any one decision because the staff says so. The staff is obligated to make sure the leaders consider all

options within the resources and guidelines of the organization.

3) Consequences. The final component of the staff's responsibility in volunteer decision making is to inform the leaders of the possible consequences of each option presented. For example, if the options open to the leaders are to fund a program or not fund it, then the staff should indicate what happens in each case. If the leaders decide to fund the program, the staff might say that it will require taking funds out of the organization's reserves, which will also require a vote of the Board. If, however, the decision is to not fund the program, the staff should point out that several big sponsors would likely withdraw their support of the organization.

Once the staff has done these three things - provide information, clarify options, and explain the consequences of each option - the staff has done its job. Until the staff has done this, its job hasn't been fulfilled.

Now that all of the information and input has been gathered, a vote can be taken. Before calling for a final vote, the Chair can summarize once again the pros and cons of the issue. After reassuring the committee that everyone has had a fair chance to express his or her views, the Chair can call for a vote.

A note about taking votes and reaching final decisions. It is often said that good leaders are those that can manage through *consensus*. That really depends upon the definition used for the word consensus. The dictionary defines consensus as "general agreement; a majority of opinion". That definition is the one most people accept, but in a volunteer organization consensus needs to be even more than just "majority of opinion". For volunteer leaders, the key to effectiveness is to have decision-making occur at a level where everyone *agrees to support the majority's viewpoint.*

What's the difference between these two definitions? Simply this. The first definition (a majority of opinion) means that more people agreed with the decision than disagreed with it. The second definition means that even though some of the participants didn't agree with the outcome, they do agree that once the decision is made they are obligated to support the decision. The key to this second outcome is the *process* by which the decision is made. People can accept losing a vote (they may not like it, but they can accept it) if they think they had a fair chance of having their viewpoint heard. What they can't accept is a decision in which they think their opinion wasn't given a fair chance of being heard.

One last suggestion for running effective committee meetings. Before the meeting is adjourned, the Chair (or another designated person) should very quickly review all of the decisions and all of the assignments that were made. There should be agreement by all in attendance that these were, in fact, the decisions made at the meeting. This summary serves two purposes. First, it reminds attendees of all of the work they completed and reinforces the fact that their time was well spent. Second, it assures that there are no misconceptions about who agreed to do what and who has assignments between now and the next meeting.

Facilitation skills are critical to the success of any leader. The ability to bring people together and get something done is one of the key ways that people measure leadership in others, and it is one of the most important Gifts of Leadership.

Chapter 11
Presentation Skills - You're Always "On"

Barry was sure that he had everything he needed for his presentation to the funding agency. As his organization's Treasurer, and Chair of the Finance Committee, no one knew the group's financial status and needs better than he did. He was prepared for the agency Board's questions, too. He had worked with them before and he knew they were always asking about "impact" - how many people did you serve, what was your cost per person served, what percentage of your funds goes to administration rather than to the program's recipients, etc., etc. Since Barry's group was competing for limited funding, he knew how important this presentation would be. The agency supplied nearly one-third of the group's total budget and they couldn't afford to have any of the funds cut for the coming year.

Although Barry wasn't a polished or experienced speaker, he had confidence in his ability to represent the group. His presentation at the organization's general assembly had been just fine. In fact, he thought his presentation style actually added to his credibility because he didn't come off too refined or rehearsed. That's what the members and the agency want to see, he thought to himself, a no-nonsense business person handling the organization's financial matters.

Barry was right. The agency Board was impressed with his knowledge of the group's finances and how the money was (and was going to be) spent. He had reasons for the funding agency to maintain current funding levels for the group and also to seriously consider raising the funding level for next year. He took every question from the Board and tried to turn it into a discussion, not a debate. He avoided using words such as "demand" and "crisis". He wanted the group to be considered strictly on the facts, not on emotion. Barry was crushed when the Board announced that it was cutting his group's funding by 11%.

How can that be, he wondered? Those people had all the information they needed and still came up with the wrong decision. Don't they understand how important our work is?

Still recovering from the shock of the announcement, Barry was walking to his car in the parking lot. A local t.v. station reporter and cameraman stopped him.

"Sir," the reporter started, "how does it feel to be one of only three organizations to get cut under the new budget?"

"I'll tell you exactly how I feel," Barry replied. "I'm disappointed. I feel sick. I realize that the Board has a very tough job, but they had all the facts and figures and apparently they couldn't add two and two and get four. Their decision makes no sense. It was obvious that each of the Board members had a pet project to protect, and I can understand that. It's too bad that budget cuts left us, and a couple of others, out of the bigger pot, and you can see what happened to us. Next time I'll have to spend a little less time justifying our requests through actual facts and do what some of the other groups seemed to do - say whatever the Board wants to hear."

Barry had his say, and he felt better about it - until the evening news. Much to his surprise, there he was on the local news program. Unfortunately, not ALL of his brief conversation with the reporter made it on the air. The few seconds that showed Barry's reaction were cut from his longer statement and Barry wasn't happy with the results. He looked heavy on the t.v., his face was red, and his tie was distractingly off center. The worst part, however, was the interview itself. This is what came out of Barry's "interview".

Reporter: "We're here interviewing the Treasurer of one of the three groups that received cuts in next year's agency budget. What are your feelings about this decision?"

Barry: "I'm sick. They couldn't add two and two and get four."

Reporter: "There you have it. I'd say that this is one organization that's not too happy with this particular set of Board members. Now, back to the studio."

Barry didn't have time to be upset about the news clip. His phone started ringing before the show was even off the air. The first call was from the organization's President.

"What did you mean, saying they couldn't add two and two?" he fumed. "What do you think it's going to be like trying to get money next year? They won't believe a word we say to them. WHAT were you thinking?"

Barry was devastated. All that preparation for nothing. No one told him that the agency people were going to grill him like that. And that reporter, Barry thought. He really twisted my words and made me come off as belligerent and negative.

Besides, I wasn't expecting to do a television interview. If that's what I have to put up with to be a leader in this organization, then I don't want to do it anymore.

Where had Barry gone wrong?

Nowhere, actually. Barry had simply been placed in three different situations, each of which called for different presentation skills. Barry had confidence in his ability to communicate effectively but he failed to realize that different situations call for different types of communication and a variety of presentations skills. Here are a few pointers that might have helped Barry.

Presenting to an Audience

The most common presentation situation for leaders involves standing in front of a group. This might be a group of members or supporters, it might be at a function of an allied organization or potential partner in a program, or it might be a group of citizens who are unfamiliar with the organization or an issue. Since the organization has designated the presenter as a "leader", the audience will assume that the person can talk intelligently and passionately about the organization and its programs or services. They also assume that a leader can do this effectively. That's not always the case, and the reason is simple - fear!

For several years research groups have done studies to determine the greatest fears of human beings. The most consistent fear to top the list is the *fear of speaking in public*. Most years it is far ahead of the fear of <u>death.</u> (One of the few fears to knock public speaking from the top spot on the survey is the fear of snakes. In fact, when asked to get up in front of a group to make a one minute presentation, a volunteer leader in a trade group once said "Nope. Bring on the snakes, 'cause I'm not getting up there.")

This fear of public speaking is fairly common, so organizations shouldn't be surprised when their volunteer leaders have difficulty giving an effective presentation to a group. It's important to remember, however, that the organization's leadership is, by definition, a symbol of the best the organization has to offer. The leader's image and reputation become the organization's image and reputation every time the leader(s) speaks on behalf of the group. It is in everyone's best interest to help leaders overcome the fear of speaking and train leaders to be more effective in this area. The organization benefits because a better image is projected by the effective presentations of its leaders, the individuals benefit because they take these enhanced presentation skills with them to other situations (there's that "gift" again), and the audience benefits through increased information and enjoyment. The following is an outline that can be used to help leaders prepare for making a presentation, as well as actually making the presentation.

PREPARING TO PRESENT

HAVE A CLEAR IDEA OF YOUR GOAL

There could be several different purposes for a presentation. It's important that the audience is able to understand what you're trying to get across to them. Be concise, be clear, and be consistent.

If your goal is to *impart knowledge,* let the audience know exactly what information they're supposed to have. "I want to tell you about the work of our organization" is the easiest way to let listeners know what you're going to say. It also gets them prepared to pay attention for that specific information.

If your goal is to *express an opinion* it's important that you indicate the information you're giving is just one viewpoint. There should be no confusion about the whether you are imparting facts or feelings. "Let me tell you how our group feels about that" makes it clear this is your group's opinion.

One of your goals may be to *gain audience participation.* This can be a very effective presentation technique for getting people to remember what you said. One easy way to get participation is to ask questions that require a response. "Who can share their story with us?" or "How many of you have a relative who has been through this?" are the types of questions that ask people to respond. Something as simple as raising a hand in response to one of these questions is "participation" to audience members.

If your goal is to *give some "take away" value* to the audience, then you need to remind them of what they've learned. Be sure to end with a summarization of some of your key points, i.e. "Here are three things you can do to change the situation."

Many times a presentation's goal is to get the audience to *DO something - to take some action.* If this is the case, then you must be as forceful as possible. Don't ask the audience to "consider" something, ask them to do it. Instead of "I hope that you'll consider registering soon for the election," tell them exactly what you want them to do. "Please register now!" is more honest and direct.

On occasion, you will be asked to give a presentation that will *motivate an audience.* There are several ways to do this. One way is through some sort of testimonial, i.e. "It's the best thing I've ever done." If you have credibility with the audience your own experience can motivate them.

Another important aspect of motivating an audience is creating a feeling of empathy. If the audience believes that you understand who THEY are and what's important to them, they are much more likely to respond to your message.

ORGANIZE YOURSELF FOR SUCCESS

Making a successful presentation can depend as much on what you do before your presentation as it does on what you do when you start talking. There are several things you can do during your preparation to increase your chances of making an effective presentation.

1. Know your topic

Even if you're talking on a topic that you know well, do some "research". Be ready and able to relate your topic to the specific audience you are addressing. It's also important to have current information, especially statistics. Contact someone in your organization to get an update on any areas that might come up during your presentation. Have examples ready to share with the audience.

2. Order the points you want to make

There are certain pieces of information that are critical to getting your point across to an audience, but sometimes there is limited time to present them. Try to put them in priority order so that if you don't get all of the time you want or need, you will at least get your most important points into the presentation.

State your main points clearly and forcefully, and have some method or logic to your order. Sometimes telling the audience how many points you are going to cover can get their attention and prepare them to listen (i.e. "There are three factors that will determine the outcome of this issue"). As you identify your main points, support each one with facts or examples.

3. Know your audience

If you want to make contact with the audience and show some empathy, spend some time researching your audience prior to your presentation. Find out who the attendees are, why they might be interested in what you have to say, what their backgrounds are (i.e industry or professional status), their demographic make up, how much they know about you or your topic, etc. It always helps to establish rapport by mentioning something unique to the audience early in your presentation. It shows the audience that you've taken the time to learn something about them and it makes them more receptive to your message.

PRACTICE, PRACTICE, PRACTICE

It's difficult for many people to practice a presentation in any detail because there is no way to duplicate the setting in which the actual presentation is made. Still, there are some benefits to practicing your presentation ahead of time.

Practice will allow you to *time your presentation*. This can be critical since presenters always have set time frames in which to speak. It will also help you if you are unexpectedly asked to shorten your presentation. If you have put your key points in order of importance and timed your presentation, you will have a better idea of where to shorten your presentation and by how much.

Tape recording or video recording your presentation and playing it back to yourself can be a valuable (and sometimes eye-opening) practice method. It will allow you to pinpoint weak areas in your presentation and improve such things as body language, voice inflection, etc.

Another value of practicing your presentation will be the ability to *memorize the most important parts of the presentation* and to *use notes sparingly.* This allows you to keep eye contact with the audience during these important parts of the presentation. It creates the image of real conviction in what you are saying.

Once you are prepared in terms of what you're going to say, knowing who your audience is, and having practiced, you need to think about the actual delivery to the group. This outline gives some tips on adding impact to a presentation.

SEVEN STEPS TO UPGRADING YOUR PRESENTATION SKILLS

Step #1 - REMEMBER THAT THE INTRODUCTION IS THE FIRST PART OF YOUR PRESENTATION

Your introduction to your audience is really the beginning of your presentation. The real purpose of an introduction is to get the audience interested and excited about what you are going to say. Get your presentation off to a good start by putting some thought into your introduction.

Write your own introduction. Don't leave it to someone else to decide how you should be introduced. Only you can give your introduction the emphasis you want.

Give it to your introducer well in advance. Help the introducer do his or her job effectively. If your name or topic contains words that are difficult to pronounce, be sure to tell the introducer how to pronounce them. You can even write these words or names phonetically to assist the introducer.

Avoid "obituary" introductions, where your introduction consists <u>solely</u> of a listing of what you've done in the past. Focus on items that reinforce your qualifications to present this topic to this audience. Be sure to remind the introducer to say your name last and to lead the applause.

Step #2 - MAKE YOUR OPENING COMMENTS WORTH REMEMBERING

You get one chance to get off to a good start in your presentation, so think about the beginning of your program carefully. If you can get the audience's attention through an effective opening there is a greater chance to maintain interest and get your point across. There are several specific techniques that can be used to get a presentation off to a good start.

Instead of making an opening statement, try *asking a question.* This makes the audience respond (at least mentally). A rhetorical question such as "Have you ever wanted to go to the moon?" gets people thinking and waiting for you to make the connection between the question and your topic.

Sometimes *citing a statistic* at the outset of your presentation can get the attention of the audience. Statistics create images in people's minds and allow the presenter to use those images to get people involved in the presentation. An example of an attention-getting statistic might be "35% of all Americans are overweight". As with any opening technique, you need to be sure to show the relationship between the statistic and your topic.

A frequently used opening is *a quote* that makes a point or helps the group relate to your topic. Often a quote with which the audience is familiar (i.e. Ben Franklin said "A penny saved is a penny earned") can establish rapport and get the attention of the listeners.

Step #3 - BE AWARE OF THE IMPORTANCE OF PHYSICAL APPEARANCE AND DELIVERY

When you get the opportunity to represent your organization in front of a group you should use all of the tools available to you to make it an effective presentation. Your own personal appearance and delivery style will become a symbol of your organization to your audience.

Speak in a confident tone and try to project the image that while you may be nervous you strongly believe in what you are saying. If you appear too polished you can lose your credibility with some audiences.

Look at the audience, not your notes, as much as you can. You needn't memorize your entire speech verbatim, but eye contact is important to get response from the audience. *Use voice inflection* to emphasize key points, and *use body language* to break things up and to express enthusiasm.

Step #4 - KEEP WITHIN YOUR TIME FRAME

When you keep your presentation within the allotted time, you *show respect* for the audience and those who asked you to speak. Be sure to reconfirm your time allotment prior to your presentation. If there is a speaker on before you, it's also a good idea to sit in on that presentation to avoid repetition and overlap.

Step #5 - IF APPROPRIATE, TRY TO GET AUDIENCE
    INVOLVEMENT

People tend to remember a presentation longer and in more
detail if they have been involved in the presentation in some
way. Not all presentations are appropriate for audience
participation, but it is a good idea to get SOME reaction from
the audience if possible. Here are a few suggestions for
gaining audience participation.

Ask the audience to *share an experience or opinion with
someone else in the audience.* This can be as simple as asking
the audience to talk to the person next to them to gain
another viewpoint on a topic. This promotes *physical
interaction* and breaks up the presentation.

Since not everyone is comfortable raising his or her hand and
asking a question in public, *get questions in writing* either
before or during your presentation. The questions can be
anonymous if that will encourage greater participation.

Poll the audience on one or more questions. Ask how many
feel a certain way or have shared a common experience. The
raising of hands in response to the polling is another way to
get attendees physically involved in the presentation.

Have a question and answer period at the end of your
presentation. Be certain that you are clear about whether or
not the question and answer period is part of your total
presentation time or is allotted in addition to it.

Step #6 - SHOW THE AUDIENCE YOU CARE ABOUT THEIR
    INPUT

If you make the effort to get input and participation from the
audience, it's important to make them feel that you really

value that input. There are a number of ways to do this.

Repeat key points given by the questioner. Repeating specific words or phrases shows that you have listened to the question.

Write thoughts on an overhead or flip chart. When people see their thoughts in writing they feel that the speaker is paying attention and telling others about their input.

Make eye contact with the audience. Show that you can listen as well as talk.

Step #7 - MAKE THE CLOSING AS FORCEFUL AS THE OPENING

When you are ready to end your presentation, be sure to bring it to a close in a way that will help the audience remember what you said.

Be sure to *thank the appropriate people.* This includes the host/sponsor, the person who introduced you, and the audience.

Summarize important conclusions and points once again before you close. This will reinforce the information you wanted to get across to the audience.

Let them know you're finished. Be sure that there is an obvious ending to your program.

Refer back to one of your opening comments in your closing. It brings the presentation full circle and reinforces the important points you made at the beginning.

One of the biggest concerns of leaders in a speaking situation is whether or not to use humor in their presentations. There's an old saying among professional speakers that says "Humor is always appropriate, but it's not always appropriate humor." That's a very good guideline to follow. The telling of jokes should be left to professional comedians. Crude, off-color humor is never acceptable. If a speaker uses a humorous anecdote in a presentation, it should relate directly to the theme of the presentation. Using humor out of context is a sure way to confuse an audience and distract them from what you came to tell them.

The idea of training leaders to be better presenters is NOT to make professional speakers out of them. If volunteer leaders put a priority on style over substance they lose a lot of the credibility they bring with them to the presentation. The goal is to help sincere, believable leaders do a better job of getting their message across and helping the organization accomplish its goals.

Talking to the Media

Speaking to the media requires different skills and approaches. First, remember in dealing with the media that they can only use your information if it meets their needs. Newspapers need a story that is either of national or international importance (which is probably not what your organization has to offer) or something that relates to a person or people within their readership area. This second need is the one you and your organization can probably fulfill.

Speaking to television reporters is another matter. T.V. people need information that can be communicated to an audience in a matter of seconds (or, if you're very lucky, minutes). That's all the time any story is going to get, so they want a story that is easy to tell and has some meaning to viewers. Again, having a story that involves local people will get more interest from television reporters.

The key to being successful in speaking to the media is to be prepared. You never know when an opportunity is going to come up. Here are some general tips for speaking to the media.

1) Have an organizational policy on who is to represent the organization with the media. Media relations is an important factor in an effective organization and it shouldn't be a victim of management by assumption.

2) Have a few basic statements ready at all times. These statements should be the type that identify your organization and present your basic message in a few words or phrases.

3) Be patient. Remember that media representatives are trained to draw out information and get people to say provocative things. Don't lose your patience because they don't seem to be paying attention to your side of a story.

4) Don't let your ego get in the way. Many people like seeing themselves on television or seeing their names in the paper. If you are representing your organization as a leader be sure that the organization's story gets across, not just your story.

5) When dealing with television reporters, reword each question you get in the first part of your answer. This makes it difficult for the technicians to take your statements out of context.

6) Try to put your organization's story in the context of something that is current in the field or in the community.

Speaking to the media presents a great opportunity to get your organization's point of view out to the largest possible audience. To take advantage of this opportunity, know what you want to say, keep your composure, and give your story relevance.

Testifying - A Special Speaking Skill

Some organizations have one or more public agencies they are trying to influence. These agencies could be elected officials (i.e. legislative bodies) or appointed officials (i.e. regulatory bodies and funding agencies). Opportunities to present an organization's viewpoint to these agencies will usually have some sort of time limit on them. This means there is great pressure to get your message across clearly and quickly. Here is a brief guide that can aid those who are testifying before these various agencies or boards.

1. Remember Your Goal Is to Communicate a Message

Concentrate on your audience. Making eye contact with the officials and showing interest in their comments and questions is a sure way to gain credibility and respect from those you are trying to influence.

Come prepared with two texts - one short and one long. It is very common for hearings and other forums to become lengthy and detailed. An organization that can be succinct in its presentation can get support just through the ability to be brief.

Talk to experienced people and get input on your testimony. If you've never appeared before an agency or Board it can be an intimidating experience. Learn as much as you can about the members of the group which will be hearing your testimony. Find out who these people are and what they want to learn from you.

2. Know What's Expected of You

Pay attention to the specific protocol of the agency or organization. There are certain rules and ways of doing things that are unique to each group.

Make your points coherently and concisely. Try to be positive about everything you present.

3. Remember to Do Your Homework

Know the issues that are involved. You should also know the other side of the issue as well as you know your own. Know the specifics of the bill, statute, law, ordinance, etc. in question, and refer to them in your presentation.

Be sure to rehearse your testimony. Timing, voice inflection, and clarity are critical factors in getting your point across.

4. The Testimony

Your actual testimony should be simple, well organized, and well documented. While trying to be logical and direct, there is nothing wrong with adding some colorful or quotable comments into your testimony. Sometimes a phrase that your listeners can remember will make your testimony stand out from that of others.

Always try to be _for_ something, rather than against something. Be certain that written testimony which accompanies your verbal testimony is submitted on time.

5. Accomplishing Your Goal

When you testify, state your position and your argument forcefully. CLEARLY identify exactly what action you want the officials to take (fund a program, support a piece of legislation, etc.). Describe what will be accomplished if the action you're requesting is taken (more people served, safer conditions, etc.).

Effective presentation skills are critical to the success of every leader in every field. This is especially true of leaders in volunteer organizations. Their organizations compete for the attention and support of the public, government officials, funding sources, communities, etc. The image presented by the organization's spokespeople becomes the organization's image, too. To make that image a positive one, one that instills a real desire for individuals, companies, and institutions to support the organization, spokespeople have to make a good first impression. Organizations can leave that first impression to chance, or they can make that first impression a positive one by giving leaders the gift of presentation skills' training.

Chapter 12 - Delegation Skills

Everyone Needs Some Help Sometimes

Charlie really liked being a committee chair for his organization. He had run the annual trade show for six years, yet each year it seemed like he had less and less help. Still, he pretty much had the show routine down to a science. He drew up the floor plans, worked with the meeting site, used his computer to make up the sales brochure, sent the brochure to all of the previous exhibitors, and arranged for the sponsors. As the Chair he also made a lot of the follow up calls to the potential exhibitors to sell the floor space. It was a fairly small show and the exhibits tended to be table top displays rather than big, free standing ones. That enabled Charlie to manage things on show day - getting the hall set up, walking around and talking to the exhibitors, making sure that all of the little things were under control. After six years, he knew most of the exhibitors personally and could handle the majority of their problems. Yes, running the show was a lot of work but it sure felt good after it was completed. The organization counted on the show income to make certain that its budget was met for the year and Charlie took pride in running the show in a way that maximized profit.

This year Charlie decided he didn't want to work so hard, and he was going to get some help. He called a couple of the people on his committee but they thought he was joking. He had planned the whole thing, they told him, so they assumed he was going to run the whole thing just like he always did. Finally, Charlie was able to get three other people to help.

The day of the show Charlie really got frustrated. He told the three volunteers what to do but they didn't really know exactly what he wanted. They kept asking him questions and Charlie just didn't have time to answer all of them and still run the show. What's more, although he had the three committee members to help him, Charlie didn't seem to think the show ran as smoothly as it did the previous year. A couple of the exhibitors even mentioned to him that they felt some of the usual efficiency was missing. Charlie decided that no one could run the show as well as he could. He didn't want the quality of "his" show to go down, and he didn't want to work that hard anymore. So he called the organization's president and said that this would have to be his last show.

The problem for the organization was that they had no one to take over. Charlie running the show had become an organizational tradition, an institution of its own. Where would they find a new chair?

Sometimes in volunteer organizations leaders really do get "attached" to their jobs. As was mentioned earlier, this frequently happens when volunteers gain something from their volunteer experience that isn't available in other areas of their lives. They cling to their volunteer leadership role because it gives them not only a sense of accomplishment but a sense of security. The problem for the organization comes when these people won't - or can't - let go of their assigned roles. It keeps the group from making the best use of its resources and it stops the organization from developing the next "generation" of leaders. Charlie may have had a lot going for him - dedication, tradition, a record of success, etc. - but he lacked one of the most important skills of leadership, the ability to **delegate**.

The Importance of Delegation

Delegation skills are important to volunteer leaders for a variety of reasons which are directly tied to the success of the organization.

1) Delegation releases time for managing

It is impossible for a leader to keep focused on the group's goals if he or she is tied down doing all of the work necessary to accomplish those goals. The job of the leader is to make certain that the work being done is in line with the organization's stated objectives. This means that leaders need to spend a large percentage of their time coordinating the work of others and helping others understand the value of their input to the organization.

2) Delegation relieves pressure

If leadership gets to be too much of a burden no one wants to be a leader. By delegating appropriate tasks to others effective leaders take some of the "performance" pressure off themselves without taking away the ultimate responsibility of getting the work completed.

3) Delegation develops other leaders

Getting others involved in leadership is a way of giving them the Gift. The delegation of challenging tasks, tasks that take advantage of the skills of others, is the way to get them started toward the Gift.

4) Delegation increases results

The basic reason delegation is a necessity in most organizations is the simple need to share the work load. More gets done if more people are involved. In addition, people who are involved in doing the work of the organization are much more committed to seeing the work through to a successful conclusion.

Why Don't People Delegate?

There are usually a number of reasons why people are reluctant to delegate. These reasons may fall into one of the following categories:

1) They're afraid the work won't get completed.
2) They're afraid the work won't get completed in time.
3) They're afraid the work WILL get completed and then they won't be needed.
4) They're afraid the work won't get completed the right way.
5) They're afraid the work won't get completed the way they would do it themselves.

By the way, number 4 (getting the work completed the right way) and number 5 (getting it completed my way) are often considered the same by the delegator.

Since some people have a need to feel indispensable, these reasons for not delegating may seem reasonable. Of course, no one person is indispensable to an organization. The organization needs to continue its work regardless of the individuals involved. This is another reason delegation is so critical to volunteer organizations. If the organization does become dependent on one or two key people, it risks losing continuity and a cadre of experienced leaders to call upon. Effective delegation is the way to bring these future leaders along, but *effective* delegation means more than just giving others something to do.

Step 1 - Know Your Workers

If leaders and organizations are constantly taking a resource check, then they have some idea of what skills their people have. Remember, one of the ways to get people interested in leadership is to give them a feeling that their talents are being used.

Step 2 - Communicate CLEARLY

It's important that when assignments are made the person giving the assignment takes his or her time to be certain that the person spoken to understands the assignment. The delegator needs to be specific about what is expected. "Get some information about the project back to the Board" isn't sufficient. "Report back at the next Board meeting on the three biggest problems you anticipate in completing this project under budget" is a different way of saying the same thing and assuring that the person has a clearer idea of what is expected.

Step 3 - Ask the Person to Repeat the Assignment

This sounds like a demeaning exercise for the delegator and the assigned person, but it is the one sure way to be certain the person really understands the assignment. If the person can't repeat the assignment accurately, there needs to be some further discussion about what is expected.

Step 4 - Delegate, Don't Abdicate

When delegating to others it's important that leaders don't give the impression they are doing someone a favor. Leaders need to be sincere in letting others know that a team effort is needed to be successful, and that each person is making a meaningful contribution.

Step 5 - Delegate Challenging Work

Leaders should be careful not to delegate only those tasks that they don't want to do or like to do. As difficult as it may be, leaders should delegate tasks that challenge other people's abilities. This will give people a greater sense of accomplishment. It may also mean other people will fail some of the time, but sometimes failure is a great teacher.

Step 6 - Set Time Frames for Progress Review

Even with the smallest of tasks, it pays to establish time frames for checking progress. Rather than the delegator arbitrarily checking up on others, there should be some preestablished times at which the leader and the assigned person will discuss progress. This could be as simple as a quick phone call or, if necessary, a meeting.

Step 7 - Give Credit, Absorb Blame

The truly effective leader will also remember that recognition for a job well done is the second most important aspect of working for someone else. It is also the new leader's paycheck. The delegator needs to be willing to give as much credit as possible to others who help the organization. The leader should accept as much blame as is reasonable when the delegated person isn't as successful as everyone would like.

Delegation is a great skill to have, and an even greater one to give. Part of the Gift of Leadership is the ability to make others successful. It's a skill - and a gift - that leaders can use in their personal and professional lives.

Chapter 13 - Top Level Management Skills

Keeping the Eyes on the Prize

The monthly meeting of the Board of Directors was about to begin. Janis was hoping that this meeting would go faster than the last three had. The problem was the Board had so much work to do it took a lot of time to get through everything on the agenda. Overall, Janis thought that Judy, the President, ran a pretty good meeting and kept things moving along. The Board was so active and involved - which was good - that everyone felt a little overwhelmed by all the decisions that had to be made at each meeting. Well, Janis thought, better to have a hard working, concerned Board than just one or two people trying to do everything.

Judy opened the meeting with a request. "As you know, we've got a very full agenda today, so I'd really appreciate it if we can keep focused on each topic and not get sidetracked. I'll try not to cut off any pertinent discussion but we do need to get through everything today. Thank you."

Perfect, thought Janis. Judy's just as worried about the length of these meetings as everyone else. Maybe we'll get out of here on time.

Judy proceeded with the meeting. "First thing on the agenda is the minutes from the previous meeting. You all received a copy of these last month. Can I have a motion to approve?"

"Thanks. Now, next is our monthly financial report from our treasurer. Alex, can you please give your report?"

"Thanks, Judy. You all have a copy of the monthly report in your packets. I'll give you a few minutes to look through them and then I'll answer any questions."

Bill spoke up. "Alex, I noticed on the expense statement that we spent $1,000 on that speaker at the convention. I really didn't think that speaker was all that good. Why did we spend so much?"

"I'd have to agree with you, Bill," said Alex. "I didn't think that guy was much good either. Maybe Jim can tell us why he cost $1,000."

Jim, the Executive Director, was caught a little off guard. "I think that the speaker fee was discussed at length at the meeting before the convention. You were the ones that o.k.'d the expenditure."

Bill jumped in. "While we're on the expenses, I see here under the attachments that we had an American Express charge from last month for a hotel room and meals for the Exec in the capital. How come the Board didn't get an itemized statement? I don't know about you all, but I sure can't afford to stay at these kinds of hotels, and I get a little concerned when someone who works for us stays at them on my nickel."

Janis was beginning to realize that this was going to be another long night.

Judy tried to control things. "I'll tell you what. I'm going to ask the Executive Director to get back to us on these items at the next meeting. We really do need to move on. The next item is the replacement for our receptionist. Jim, where do we stand?"

Jim said "I've narrowed the search down to three people."

Judy interjected, "Jim, that's great. Why don't you pass around the resumes to the Board members and we can discuss them one by one."

After 25 minutes of discussion, the Board voted to recommend hiring candidate number two. Then one of the Board members brought up the salary. "I just hired a receptionist at our place, so I have a pretty good idea what they're making. We paid the last receptionist way too much compared to the average out there in the market place. Just because the last one made that much doesn't mean that this next one should. I think we ought to offer her $500.00 less than the budget amount and give it to her as a bonus after 6 months or so if she works out."

This prompted a lengthy discussion on the merits of paying top dollar up front to attract the right people versus trying to keep costs down. Eventually the Board voted to pay the receptionist the full budgeted amount but to tell her she wouldn't be eligible for a raise until after she had been there a year.

"Well," Judy stated, "I guess that settles that. Jim, what's next on the agenda?"

Before the discussion could continue, Janis decided that she had had enough. She stood up and got everyone's attention.

"Hold it, hold it, hold it. I've been coming to these meetings for several months now, and I have to say that I'm confused. I agreed to serve on this Board because we had some important things to do and some important decisions to make. But when

I come to these meetings we seem to spend a lot of time on things that aren't even on the agenda. What exactly are we doing here?"

Great question, Janis.

If the challenge of leadership is to identify and maximize resources, then wasting those resources is one of the biggest mistakes leaders can make. As volunteers move up the leadership ladder toward the level at which they are making important decisions, they need to learn the difference between *doing things* and *getting things done*. Doing things means putting in the time and effort to do the work of the organization. That work could include managing a committee, fund raising, heading up a task force, or getting out and recruiting members. Certainly these are among the most important functions in an organization and all volunteers want and need to do these jobs. The role of the Board (the governing body of the organization, whatever title it has), however, isn't to do the work. It's to get the work done. In order for that to happen, the Board needs to focus its resources on deciding what is best for the organization. There are six key areas on which the Board should be focused: financial management; planning; policy; resource development; staff and committee support; and promotion.

Financial Management

In every sense - legally, ethically, administratively - the Board is responsible for the financial well-being of the organization. This doesn't mean that each person on the Board needs to be a financial wizard or have knowledge of accepted accounting procedures. The organization has to be certain that the financial assets of the organization are being handled by competent people, but most of the time there are people outside of the organization who can do this. Even in cases where successful business people and financial professionals sit on Boards there is more to financial management than being able to read the financial statements. Effective financial management entails making sure that the organization's financial resources are being spent in the most efficient manner. The organization should be led by people who are committed to making the most impact with whatever resources exist, and this is the true financial responsibility of the Board. It isn't simply a matter of dollars and cents - it's a matter giving the loudest possible voice to the people and causes that the organization represents. Effective financial management should be one of the priorities of the Board.

Planning

In the musical "South Pacific", there is a song called "Happy Talk" that is sung by the character Bloody Mary. The chorus in the song goes "You got to have a dream, if you don't have a dream, how you gonna have a dream come true?" If that sounds a little silly it really does tell the basic story of why planning is important to any organization. The planning process assures that the organization has a real idea not only of where it wants to go but how it intends to get there.

Of all the responsibilities of the Board, planning is perhaps the most important. If the Board is not focusing on the future, then no one is. In fact, this focus on the future, of ways to improve the organization, accomplish its mission, and increase its impact, is really the *permanent agenda* of the Board. The plan should identify where the organization is going and the Board needs to monitor the group's progress toward its goals. The plan should also include some measurement criteria, which can determine if the plan is working, and if the organization is on track.

In many organizations, the strategic or long range plan is a document that the leadership reviews once every couple of years. In fact, the plan is supposed to be a management tool for the organization's volunteer and staff leaders. If the plan is developed effectively, everything that goes on in the organization should be designed to help accomplish one or more of the objectives set out in the plan. By accomplishing those objectives (as measured by the criteria established in the plan) the organization should be moving toward a more effective representation of its constituency.

Here is an example of how one organization formatted a part of their plan:

Mission
The Mission of the organization is to improve the quality of life for physically challenged citizens.

Vision
Our vision is to create a barrier free, discrimination free environment that provides physically challenged people equal opportunities in the workplace and in society.

Areas of Concentration
To make this vision a reality by the beginning of the 21st century, we will focus our resources in the following areas:

1) Public awareness
2) Legal and regulatory support
3) Membership and fundraising
4) Leadership development
5) Communications
6) Building alliances

Measuring Success
Our success in each of these areas will be measured in the following ways:

Area of Concentration
Public Awareness

Objective
To make the public aware of the needs and concerns of physically challenged citizens

Measurement Criteria
1) # of favorable news articles
2) # of attendees at organization-sponsored programs
3) # of times we are called on for information and/or testimony

This is just a sample of what a plan can show. It is important for the organization that the leadership (i.e. the Board) believes the plan is a road map for success. If that is the case, then this format can help the Board focus its effort. Each activity, program, or service sponsored by the organization should relate to the accomplishment of one or more of the group's objectives and should be measurable by one or more of the criteria listed in the plan.

Setting Policy
Most people recognize the fact that Boards are usually responsible for establishing policy. This is one of the few responsibilities that is almost always spelled out in an organization's by-laws or charter. Boards should also remember that in addition to establishing policy they are responsible for assuring that policies are implemented and followed by all of the representatives of the organization (committees, staff, etc.).

One of the most difficult challenges for Board members in the area of policy making is to remember that they (the Board members) represent others who are not present when these policies are established. Each Board member brings a certain amount of personal opinion into the Board's discussion. Board members need to think about who or what they represent - members, supporters, the recipients of the organization's work - as well as what they think or feel personally. One advantage of the group decision making process is the ability to adequately represent the entire spectrum of the organization. Boards should be careful not to lose this advantage by setting policy based on what is good for the individual rather than what is good for the organization.

Resource Development

The Board isn't just responsible for spending the organization's money, it's also responsible for helping raise the money. Not all Board members want to be personally involved with membership and fund raising. Some are not comfortable with the sales aspect of membership or soliciting contributions from peers and acquaintances.

The reason Board members don't get actively involved in helping the organization grow is that they weren't told that was part of their responsibility when they accepted the leadership position. This is a classic case of management by assumption. It was assumed that if a person agreed to serve in a leadership role at the Board level the person would know that fund raising and/or membership was part of the leadership responsibility. This is a bad assumption. If an organization expects its Board members to be actively involved in funding activities then it has an obligation to tell leaders of this expectation before they assume their role on the Board. It's very awkward to complain about the lack of Board participation in funding activities if no one on the Board knew that this was expected.

To overcome the reluctance of some Board members to actually do membership or fund raising work, one organization came up with a system that requires Board members to help the organization grow but is flexible enough to allow each Board member to participate in a way that is comfortable. This organization designed a "point" system for Board members in the area of organizational growth. Rather than insisting on direct membership recruitment or fund raising as the criteria for meeting Board requirements, the group asked Board members to commit to earning a minimum number of "growth points" each year they served on the Board. These points could be earned by sponsoring a new member, calling to thank someone for a contribution, writing letters, welcoming a new member, etc. The Board member earned the most points for doing something directly related to growth, such as recruiting a new member or getting a large contribution, but they could earn points in less threatening ways, too. This system seemed to work well for this group. It got their Board to commit to thinking about growth and to actively participate in it.

Regardless of the Board members' individual or collective involvement, it is part of their job to be certain that the organization does have adequate funding.

Staff and Committee Support

The Board should be certain that there is appropriate support for the work of the organization's staff and committee structure. The Board should be careful about redoing the work already done by the committees. If the Board (as was described in the earlier example) spends its time going over committee work and redoing it to suit the desires of the Board, what was the purpose of the committee work in the first place? One of the main reasons a committee structure exists is to give the Board a way to delegate. The delegation of the work to committees is done so that the Board can accomplish *its* job, which is to <u>act on the recommendations of the committees.</u> If the committee has completed its job appropriately, it should be making recommendations to the Board on how the organization can best achieve its goals (the ones that apply to each particular committee). The committee should also be describing what specific programs, services, activities, etc. the organization should undertake to meet the goals. The Board's job is to make sure the recommendations of the committees are in keeping with the organization's policies and budget, and are in line with helping the organization implement its strategic plan. If the committee's recommendations meet these criteria, and the Board has given clear directions to the committee, then the Board shouldn't be changing the work of the committee. They should be endorsing it and supporting it in every way possible.

Supporting the work of the staff is another obligation of the Board. Again, the Board must be certain the staff understands its job and the direction of the Board. This understanding of roles and responsibilities is a joint responsibility - a responsibility to avoid management by assumption at the highest organizational levels. The Board must be willing to express its collective wishes clearly and concisely so that the staff knows how to allocate the existing resources and provide the Board with the information it needs to make accurate decisions. The staff must ask the appropriate questions to get clarification on what the Board wants and how the Board will measure adequate performance.

Promotion

A final responsibility of the Board is to actively promote the organization and its work whenever possible. This doesn't mean that each Board member should be talking to the media and trying to get the group's name in the press (that's an easy thing to do - just continue to manage by assumption). There is a big difference between publicity and promotion. Publicity can be equated with getting name recognition, but there can be both good publicity and bad publicity. Promotion means taking advantage of every opportunity to promote the positive aspects of the organization. Those opportunities are often overlooked by Board members because they don't connect the organization on whose Board they sit with some of the situations in which they find themselves. It is part of the Board member's job to make these connections and use daily contacts with other people and organizations to promote the work of the group.

This promotion can take many forms. First of all, the Board member should find every possible opportunity to let others know that he/she is a Board member. This establishes credibility as a leader and almost always leads someone to ask the person to tell them a little more about the organization. The Board member may be talking to a potential member or supporter but will never know that if affiliation with the organization, and his or her leadership position, isn't made known.

A second technique is along the same lines but more formal. Board members are frequently active in another (or several other) voluntary organization as well as the one in which they serve as Board members. These Board members often have occasions to address these other groups. They should put something in their introductions and/or resumes that notes their leadership role in the organization. This gives the audience a chance to note the person's support of the organization and again invites questions that lead to discussions of the organization's work. It's entirely possible that the Board member is addressing a *room full of potential members or supporters*, and it's an opportunity that the organization doesn't want to miss.

A last word about this Board responsibility to promote the organization. There will be occasions when a Board member will disagree with the decision made by the Board, but that person is still expected to go out and promote the organization. It would be easy for the individual to communicate his or her disagreement with the Board at the same time he or she is communicating the Board's decision. This is often, unfortunately, exactly what happens. What does this say about the organization? What does it say about the individual?

Does this mean the individual is not entitled to his or her own opinion? Certainly not. Part of the problem here is that the decision making process probably didn't work. The person expressing disagreement or disappointment with the Board's decision probably felt as though his or her viewpoint wasn't given adequate consideration when the Board reached its decision. That's why "true consensus" is so critical to the organization's decision making system. What's being put into question in this case is the Board member's integrity.

Integrity, according to the dictionary, is defined as "honesty or virtue". Another definition may fit for this particular situation. A counselor, when asked the definition of integrity by his group of teenaged charges, once said that "Integrity is what you do when no one is looking." That's really what this type of integrity is all about. It's easy for a person to attend a Board meeting and agree to go along with the group's decision while still sitting in the meeting room. The real test of the person's integrity comes when none of the other Board members are around. Is the person still going to present the Board's decision in an appropriate way? This is why the skill of effective decision making is such a great "gift" to give to Board members and other leaders.

To truly serve the needs of the organization the Board must keep its efforts focused on those things that a Board does best. That includes financial management, planning, policy making, staff and committee support, resource development, and promotion.

Part IV
Moving Ahead

Chapter 14 - Stop the Insanity, and Relight the Spirit

In rural Georgia, they've discovered that a fish they thought was extinct for over 100 years has actually been living in the local waters all the time. The fish was such a delicacy back in the days when cotton was harvested in the area that the farmers and their workers literally ate the fish out of existence - at least, that was the theory. When first one, and then several dozen, of the fish were discovered, the wildlife agency in Georgia began tracking the fish and trying to figure out how many were left and how humans might be able to help the species survive.

It turned out that almost all of the fish they found were old and large, with very few young fish around to carry on the next generation. It was estimated that if something wasn't done quickly the fish would have no chance of surviving through another generation. The wildlife agency wanted to intervene and do something to help. They wanted to try a unique method of giving hormones to the female fish to produce extra eggs, then hatch the eggs and return the young fish to their native waters to grow and, hopefully, increase their numbers for the next generation.

The wildlife people, unfortunately, had a dilemma. If they declared the fish endangered, the fish would fall under the U.S. Endangered Species Act, and all contact with the fish would be governed by thousands of pages of government regulations, hundreds of laws and rules, and level after level of bureaucratic oversight. On top of that, by the time the agency got through all the governmental processes necessary to actually DO anything to help the fish, it would have been too late. Rather than face all that, the agency decided not to declare the fish endangered and proceeded with their plan to save the fish in their own way.

What has all of this got to do with volunteer organizations and leadership? This *specific* incident may not seem to have a lot to do with volunteer organizations, but it does have a lot to do with the reasons people are more and more reluctant to give their time as volunteers and volunteer leaders. In the case of this species of fish, one government agency is afraid to ask another government agency for help because it is well known that the time and energy needed to wade through the government red tape will actually be detrimental to accomplishing something. This is indicative of how people are feeling about their volunteer leadership time. There is a growing feeling all over the world that governments are so bogged down with political motivation and inertia that getting involved just doesn't matter any more. Why volunteer to raise money to feed the homeless in America or the starving in underdeveloped nations when most of the money winds up in the hands of the governments and little of the food or shelter ever gets to the needy? Why volunteer to be a leader in an organization that is giving voice to a group if no one is listening, or even worse, they are listening but not hearing? It's not merely an economic issue where rich people don't want to volunteer to help poor people, or healthy people don't want to take on leadership roles in organizations that help the disabled. It's the lack of confidence that they will accomplish anything that keeps people from volunteering their valuable time.

So, what are volunteer leaders supposed to do? Can they throw up their hands and assume that they just won't get any more help? What happens to those who count on volunteer organizations to give them their "voice"? When the current leaders finally get burned out, what happens if there is no one to take their places?

Giving up, or giving in, is just not an option. The thing that organizations need to avoid is **insanity.** Insanity in this case doesn't mean a mental disorder. Insanity has another definition, though it's not one that can be found in any dictionary. Insanity also means "Doing the same thing over and over and expecting *different* results."

Volunteer organizations should realize that they are dealing with a different generation of leaders and potential leaders in the new century, and they have to approach these people in a different way than they did the previous generation. This doesn't mean that the studies that Huseman and Hatfield did in "And After All I've Done.." are out of date. Not at all. People still want to have a sense of accomplishment, they still want recognition, and they still want to get paid for the work they do. They still want, and deserve, The Gift. The difference is not in the needs of people but in the way they perceive them, and how organizations try to meet those needs. To attract volunteer leaders in the new century, organizations will need to concentrate on meeting these people on their own terms. This means understanding what affects people's lives and how that understanding can be used to convince people of the need to volunteer. The three areas on which volunteer organizations should concentrate are *time, technology, and access.*

The issue of time was discussed in earlier chapters. Limited time has been an issue for volunteers in every generation, and in the next century it will continue to be a major factor in the decision to serve or not to serve. For volunteer organizations to continue to attract the best people in the next century, they have to assume that time will always be an issue. The effective volunteer organization in the next century will use the other two areas - technology and access - to assure that those who do give up their valuable time will gain a sense of accomplishment.

Chapter 15 -Technology: High Tech Needs in a Low Tech Field

Ken was happy as an engineer for his company. He had job security, good working conditions, and lots of interesting projects at work. The only thing he didn't like was his daily routine.

A typical day for Ken was to get up early, do some quick exercises, grab some cereal or toast, and sneak out of the house before his wife and kids woke up. He spent 45 minutes in rush hour traffic, got to his downtown office by 7:30 am, and tried to get a few reports done before the phones started ringing. About 8:30 am the rest of the office starting filling up and the first calls came in, only to be interrupted by the morning staff meeting. After the staff meeting, Ken went back to his office to find a stack of pink "while you were out" memos and more work. He was usually on the third cup of coffee by then, and it was a rare day when he got away from the office for lunch. Afternoon meant the calls from the west coast and overseas starting to come in, further delaying Ken's attention to those reports which were the reason he came in early in the first place. He often grabbed a late afternoon snack or coffee to keep going. By about 5:30 pm (on a good day) he packed up his things and fought the rush hour traffic going home. When he finally got through the door, it was time to have dinner with the family and get the kids started on their homework. Only then did Ken catch his breath and relax for a few minutes. This schedule didn't allow much free time, but Ken found time to be an active member of his engineering society.

He enjoyed attending meetings and serving as an officer in the local chapter of his society. The volunteer time he put in was a bit of an inconvenience, but it was only one night a month for the Chapter meetings and one night a month for the leadership meetings. He enjoyed the interaction with other engineers and the chance to put something back into his profession. It gave Ken a little part of his life where he was his own boss, and he liked being an "insider".

Just when Ken thought that his life was as full as it could be, along came the "technology revolution". Ken's company thought it did him a big favor when it paid for him to have a complete computer station in his basement office at home. Ken was connected to the office computer, to the internet and World Wide Web, to electronic mail, and to his choice of any three on-line services - all at the company's expense. What was supposed to be a reward for Ken's good work and steady rise through the firm's engineering department had actually changed Ken's entire life. In Ken's view, it wasn't necessarily a change for the better.

Now Ken didn't need to worry about getting everything done at the office because he could always take it home and work on it there. After getting his kids settled down each night, Ken found himself going back down to the basement to work. Did this mean he didn't need to be in the office as early every morning? Sure. He could get up even earlier and finish the work before he went in. On weekends he could now keep ahead of those long term projects without even going into the office at all. With his on-line services and the World Wide Web he had all the information and technical assistance he needed 24 hours a day. With this ability to be productive during any spare time, Ken felt he had to give up something to take advantage of these opportunities.

He reluctantly decided it would be his volunteer time with his engineering society. He just couldn't afford those two night meetings a month plus the telephone calls in between. That was time he could spend at home with the family, and the computer. Ken gave up his leadership role, and he gave up the burdens that went with it.

He also gave up his chance to get The Gift.

Before discussing the issue of technology as it applies to volunteer leadership, there is one thing that should be made clear: *technology is not an "issue"*. It is a given. There are no sides or opinions about technology. Every organization has to deal with it from the perspective of how technology takes up people's time (i.e. Ken), how it competes for people's attention, and in some organizations, how technology competes with the organization to provide products and services to members, supporters, and the public. People who are not comfortable with technology may get tired of hearing about it and it's impact but that doesn't mean it is going away. Technology is having a tremendous impact on volunteer leadership in many ways, and it must be taken into consideration if the volunteer spirit is going to be relighted in the 21st century.

Millions of people every day are going through the same changes that Ken did. Millions more are growing up and entering the work force never knowing anything *other* than the technological side of the average workday. This generation that has grown up with the computer may have almost no experience at all in volunteer activities, except some small amount of community service mandated by a school system. How are organizations going to motivate these people to stay involved, or get involved, in volunteer leadership?

They have to use their competitive advantages. They also have to make technology work for them.

Competitive Advantages

Most volunteer organizations are unique because of the people or cause they represent. There may be other organizations that represent the same or similar constituencies, but basically this is what sets organizations apart. One of the reasons people gravitate toward these organizations is because of **information**. People want information to help them with their jobs, they want information to help them deal with a personal problem (i.e. a disease or disability, or an emotional situation), or they want information to share with others. Technology is providing major competition for every organization in the information field. When people can get information instantaneously and in great detail through their computers there is no need to attend a meeting or read a newsletter. The information is there now, and they can use it right away. If they want more information, or a better explanation of the information they already have, all they have to do is push a button.

This doesn't mean that volunteer organizations shouldn't continue providing information to members, supporters, and the public. It just means that they have to realize that their organizations are no longer the only - or even the best - source of information. They need to turn to those needs that the computer can't provide.

-The Human Touch

No on-line service, or chat room, or computer video system can truly replace the basic need people have for human contact. Volunteer organizations need to "market" leadership as a way to fulfill this need. It's not just meetings and conferences that fill this need (after all, a big part of those meetings are information). It's the work of the organization, the chance to make a difference in people's lives, and the chance to look into someone's face when you're talking to them that can be used to attract volunteers.

- Self-identification

Organizations can appeal to volunteers if they realize that more important than the fact that the *organization* is unique is the fact that the *individual* is unique. A computer can't reinforce the unique qualities and values in each person but a caring and efficient volunteer organization can.

- Affinity

People are attracted to organizations because they feel some affinity to the industry, profession, community, or cause of the organization. To get and keep a strong and active volunteer leadership base, organizations need to constantly reinforce this affinity. They also need to give people an opportunity to make a difference through personal involvement in the cause or purpose of the organization. Again, the computer can't provide this level of affinity. Volunteer organizations can not only express empathy for people, people *believe* that the organization has that empathy.

-The Gift

It is here that the volunteer organization has it's biggest advantage. Only through personal involvement can people get the Gift of Leadership. Being a talented technical person is fine but combining technical skills with leadership skills makes for a more well-rounded and fulfilled individual. The Gift also becomes a "competitive advantage" for the volunteer in the workplace and in the community. Most importantly, people possessing The Gift of Leadership will make a bigger impact and help more people.

Making Technology Work for the Organization

There are basically three types of people when it comes to dealing with the technological/computer revolution. There are the Category I people, those who have reached a state of oneness with technology and use it in every conceivable way. These are the people who are sometimes referred to as "computer geeks."

There are the Category II people, who are fairly comfortable with technology and computers and can use them to make their personal and/or professional lives more convenient and productive. These people are sometimes referred to as computer literate.

Finally, there are the Category III people, those who are hoping they can retire before all of this catches up to them. These people are referred to as "technologically challenged." These people also need to come to the realization that they didn't make it. Technology caught up to them before they were able to retire.

Technology is already a major factor in people's lives and will become even more of a factor in the future. Volunteer organizations certainly have felt the competition of technology for the time and interest of their leaders. The trick to dealing with technology in the successful volunteer organization of the next century is not to fight it but to use it.

Here are a few unique ways organizations can use technology to actually help them attract and keep volunteer leadership.

Use Technology to Recruit Volunteers

In every organization there are a certain number of Category I people. They are going to use the internet and other electronic media to get their information. Associations, social service organizations, professional societies, community action groups, youth organizations, and other types of not-for-profit and volunteer groups are a major source of information for people on a vast array of topics. Volunteer organizations can communicate with these people by using technology to get the organization's message, and it's need for volunteers, across. Why not ask the people using the internet and World Wide Web to consider becoming part of the process of making a difference (and increasing their knowledge) through volunteer leadership? This doesn't have to be just a "call for volunteers." Organizations need to be creative and use some empathy when communicating with Category I people. Instead of a general appeal for anyone who wants to help, ask for those with computer skills, or communications skills, and an interest in helping, to contact the organization via it's Home Page or fax number. Lead potential volunteers to the organization in a manner that indicates the organization is interested in using their talents, not just their time. There is even a chance to appeal to these computer literate people by telling them they can be of help to the organization without having to attend a series of meetings. They can use other means of electronic communications to help the organization with its computer needs, its publications, its Web site, and other functions.

Your Category II people can also help. These people may not be the most comfortable with technology, but some of them might enjoy using clip art and computer graphics. They can help design promotional materials, newsletters, etc. Again, the key to attracting these people to volunteer leadership isn't to ask for volunteers to put out your newsletter. The key is to appeal to people to participate in a way that allows them to feel they can <u>accomplish</u> something. That usually starts with them believing in their ability to be successful in whatever job they are given.

Use Technology to Recognize Volunteers
In the technology field, one of the hidden opportunities for volunteer organizations is the opportunity to use technology to recognize leaders for their service. Just think how rewarding it would be for your volunteers to have their name broadcast worldwide over your organization's Home Page under the category "Thanks to the following for their involvement in our organization." Organizations could update this list weekly, and people would probably start accessing the organization's web site just to see their own name, or the name of someone they know. Even better would be the e-mail and other correspondence these people would receive from people who see their names and call or write to congratulate them. It not only "pays" the volunteers for previous leadership involvement and encourages them to move to the next level of leadership, it might also raise the interest of others who like the idea of the "technological recognition" that obviously comes with participating in this particular organization.

Use Technology to Improve Quality
If there is one area that always needs improvement, it's quality control. Technology gives organizations the opportunity to improve their relationships with their various "publics" (members/supporters, the media, government entities, etc.) by enhancing their image and upgrading their communications capabilities. Technology can also be used to maintain a better and more comprehensive profile and record of volunteer leaders. Organizations can use advanced software to develop leadership resource databases. When a need arises for additional volunteer help or specific leadership talent the

organization can identify those in its database who have the talents (or the time) necessary to fill the need. Instead of hoping that someone with the right combination of skills and characteristics will come forward, organizations can pinpoint those they want to serve. This helps raise the chances of getting the right person for the right job and increases the chance for success. Technology can also be used to track follow up activities and recognition programs, to make sure that the volunteer leaders feel that there has been some closure on their work and that they gain some sense of accomplishment.

Chapter 16 - Access : Opening the Doors

Alex never felt that he needed to be part of a lot of organizations in order to get things done. He was a bit of a loner, and he felt comfortable working things out for himself. His company had grown through his hard work and innovation, and he had a trusted group of managers with many years of experience. In fact, the company that Alex had started was considered by most people to be the leading firm in the industry. Alex felt that his company really didn't have any competition - his company was the biggest and the most profitable in its field. He never saw any reason why he should have to get involved in a lot of business and professional organizations. They were a waste of time, Alex felt, with all the meetings and time away from work. Not only that, these groups were always looking for more money or sponsorships or contributions of some sort. Sure, his competitors were all active in one of the trade groups, but it seemed to Alex that they spent a lot of their time working on things that really didn't help a big company like his. Those smaller companies might need to pool their resources to get things done, but Alex didn't. His reputation and his contacts opened lots of doors, so why should he give his advantages away to others? If his managers and some of his other people wanted to participate on behalf of the company, that was o.k. with Alex. He just didn't want his people spending a lot of time on volunteer committees and Boards when they needed to be at work. If they participated, he wanted it to be on their own time, not the company's.

Alex learned in one dramatic moment how much he needed the others in his industry. When Alex wanted to expand his company's manufacturing facilities, the city council decided that they didn't want to have any more industrial sites within their area, so they refused to give Alex his building permit. When Alex tried to explain to the council how important it was to his company, he was met by a very unimpressed council. They weren't willing, they told him, to make an exception for his company just so he could make more money. In the council's opinion there wasn't anything special about the request from Alex. If it were a situation that affected the entire community, they might be more willing to listen.

Alex didn't know where to turn. He thought all of his years as head of a large company should get him some special treatment but it didn't work out that way. One of his managers suggested he contact the industry's trade group.

Alex met with their leaders, and they agreed to help him. The group arranged to use their volunteer committees to put together a presentation to the council about the need for industrial expansion. Instead of just Alex and his company asking for a change, now there was an entire business community asking the council to listen to their input.

When the city council members asked to have a meeting with a select committee of industry leaders, the trade group invited Alex to be part of their committee. The very same council members who didn't want to listen to him in his role as President of a company were now giving him all of their attention when he was representing a voluntary organization. The volunteer organization had certainly given a greater voice to Alex and his company. It also showed Alex that being the biggest doesn't always give you the credibility you think it does. Sometimes you have to find new ways to gain access to people or institutions.

The third way to appeal to volunteer leaders is using the organization's advantage in the area of **access**. Access refers to the ability of the organization to put its volunteer leaders in touch with people, organizations, and institutions that they otherwise would be unable to access. This is another opportunity for volunteer organizations to overcome the challenge of technology. People can access information through the internet but they can't access other people. They can't access the leadership of other organizations, they can't access public officials, and they can't access the interpersonal relationships they get through volunteer activities.

Some people are going to be attracted to leadership if they are convinced that the leadership experience will open doors for them. Even the CEO's of major corporations (people like Alex) can't get in to see some public officials simply because of their position within an industry or community. However, if that same person is representing a volunteer organization as a leader, there is every possibility that that same door will be open. That's why the biggest companies and the leading professionals still want their "voice" heard through organizations. Is this a selfish reason to volunteer? Perhaps, but the organization benefits from the experience and leadership of some very talented people. That level of leadership almost always means the organization can help more people through effective programs and efficient management.

It's not just these "industry" people who look for access through organizations. Many individuals gain recognition and a sense of accomplishment through meeting and associating with people in positions of influence in their communities. If this sounds like "snob appeal", that may be somewhat true. Again, what difference does it make? If talented people are attracted to leadership for the prestige of being seen with or interacting with people in positions of power, then that's fine.

At least the resources these people bring to the organization are being used to further the organization's purposes. What's more, however talented these people might be, there is still the chance for them to get The Gift of Leadership.

When top level executives have a good experience with a volunteer organization it can lead to several other very positive things. The leader will almost certainly tell others - his or her peers - about the situation. This will encourage others to get involved. It also gets the leader thinking about having others from his or her company or organization get involved. If nothing else, it makes the leader more receptive to the appeals of other organizations and (perhaps) more generous in giving financial support and time.

Chapter 17 - The Light at the End of the Tunnel

With all of the challenges that face volunteers and volunteer organizations in a modern society it would be easy to think that the future looks bleak. There will be less time for people to spend volunteering. The technological advances that are supposed to make our lives easier are really just making it possible for people to work more hours in more ways. How are organizations going to convince people to give up their time in this future environment when that time will seem even more precious?

Despite these potential challenges, there is no reason to believe that the volunteer spirit is in danger of being extinguished anytime in the very near future. There are still millions of people who are more than willing to get involved in helping "to give voice to" others. The danger really isn't in having the volunteer spirit extinguished, it's in having it die from lack of fuel. The next generation of leaders and volunteers needs to grasp the importance of continuing the tradition of giving that has made volunteer organizations so critical in the improvement of people's lives. With all of the distractions that the new century is likely to bring into everyday life, volunteer organizations will need to prove the value of participation in ways that they have never before had to do.

Each generation of leaders has a different viewpoint on what volunteering is all about. There is a whole generation of people who started participating in volunteer organizations because of a belief in the basic principals of an organization and/or the belief in the need for volunteering. Many of these people have stayed active as volunteers because they were able to gain a sense of accomplishment and, to some extent, the Gift of Leadership. These people are not going to stop believing in the value of volunteering but these people are eventually going to have to give way to another group of volunteer leaders. There are some signs that this next generation is being brought along:

- In many school systems, community service is being included as part of the required curriculum for students. This program introduces young people to the volunteer aspects of society and opens them up to new ideas about how things get done and how important volunteers and volunteer organizations really are. Part of this mandatory community service experience for students is exposure to The Gift of Leadership. They start to work with others, they are put into leadership and decision-making situations, and they gain a better perspective on the needs of the community. These experiences help them as they move on in their lives and give them a frame of reference that makes them more open to serving in a volunteer capacity as they get older.

- The concept of mentoring has been adopted by many volunteer organizations. By assigning specific experienced leaders to guide people who are new to the organizations, thousands of groups have assured a new generation of leaders that are getting a more structured introduction into the challenges and rewards of volunteer leadership. These mentors are giving the new leaders the Gift of Leadership by sharing their expertise and experience, and they are also inspiring the newer leaders by telling them about their own belief in the work of their organization. Many of these mentors are also leaders outside of the volunteer organization, in trades, professions, or the community. The fact that successful people are not only volunteering their valuable time but are taking the extra step to mentor new leaders is a wonderful sign to the new leaders about the value of volunteering. The new leaders must think that if these leaders in their fields also find value in volunteering then there must be something worthwhile gained through the volunteer leadership experience.

- In several countries, including the United States, governments are promoting the concept of volunteering as a vital factor in helping improve the quality of life. The leaders of these governments are trying to explain to their constituents that no government has the resources to "give voice to" every single one of its citizens. If the needs and wishes of all people are to be heard then volunteers need to go out and work in the community to help those who otherwise wouldn't be represented. Volunteer organizations have always had the ability to play a major role in helping advance society, so even if these governmental calls for volunteer service are somewhat belated they are still helpful in raising the consciousness of a new group of volunteers and potential volunteer leaders. If governments are going to help drive the opportunity for more people to receive the Gift of leadership then this is an important trend.

- The Gift of Leadership is being "exported" to developing democracies around the world. The U.S. government and several private foundations are working together to train people throughout the world in the art of volunteer leadership. The ability to institutionalize nongovern-mental and volunteer organizations in the early stages cf the formation of these new democracies is a wonderful opportunity for these countries to be certain that their citizens will have strong and effective voices in the future of the nations. It also ensures that volunteer organizations will be available to serve as a training ground for future leaders in all aspects of society.

The ability of volunteers and volunteer organizations to thrive in the next century is not a question of numbers. There are certainly enough people who will be available to fill the needed leadership roles. The challenge is one of making sure that the potential leaders in this new generation really understand the value and importance of volunteering. They need to realize that taking on a volunteer position in an organization will give them a true sense of accomplishment. They need to understand that there actually is "a paycheck" for the volunteer work that they do through the recognition they receive. Most importantly, they need to understand that volunteering can be more that just a challenge and more than just a burden. They need to understand that they can also receive The Gift of Leadership.

NOTES